THE MYSTICAL CRYSTAL

By the same author

The Healing Crystal (Cassells 1989)
Atlantis (The Atlantis Electronic Publishing
Association 1995)
Crystal Healing Configurations
(The Atlantis Electronic Publishing Association 1995)

GEOFFREY KEYTE

THE MYSTICAL CRYSTAL

Expanding your crystal consciousness

Index compiled by
Lyn Greenwood

SAFFRON WALDEN
THE C.W. DANIEL COMPANY LIMITED

First published in Great Britain in 1993
by The C.W. Daniel Company Limited
1 Church Path, Saffron Walden
Essex, CB10 1JP, England

© Geoffrey Keyte 1993

ISBN 0 85207 269 4

Revised Edition 1996

Designed by Tim McPhee
Produced in association with
Book Production Consultants, Cambridge
Typeset in Baskerville by Rowland Phototypesetting Limited,
Bury St Edmunds, Suffolk and printed by
St Edmundsbury Press Limited, Bury St Edmunds, Suffolk.

Since writing my previous book, *The Healing Crystal*, my family has experienced several major crises and bereavements.

Without the love and support of my wife, Judith, and my children – Seth, Tristan, Gregor and Cameron, I would not have been able to produce this new book,
The Mystical Crystal.

I am therefore dedicating this book to my wife and children in grateful thanks for all their patience and love when times have been tough.

Into every life a little crystal shall fall.

Contents

Acknowledgements

This book has been produced with the help of many people throughout the world.

Special thanks must go to Gillian Bull from the Isle of Man, Jenny Khan, and Frank Eastwood; all of whom supplied me with additional information for this book.

Thanks must also go to my good friend Bryan Talbot, who took so many excellent photographs that we had great difficulty deciding which ones to include. Thanks too to Kate Wain and Becky Byles, the 'patients' in the photographs.

I am indebted to Ian Miller of the C. W. Daniel Co Ltd, for allowing me to quote from some of his authors' books, for giving me great encouragement and for being brave enough to publish this book.

I would also like to thank all my crystal healing colleagues and friends – too numerous to mention personally – who have attended my workshops, seminars and courses during the last few years and who have, one way and another, contributed to much of the knowledge and ideas that I have expressed in this book.

Geoffrey Keyte
St Annes-on-Sea
February 1993

Prologue

Many of you will have read my first book, *The Healing Crystal*. It was extremely encouraging that a substantial number of copies found their way on to library shelves up and down the country. I understand from the Society of Authors that several thousand people each year have borrowed the book from their local library. It is very heartening to think that my humble words are reaching an ever-widening audience of seekers after the truth.

Since *The Healing Crystal* was first published in June 1989 my own range of experience has gained increasing momentum. Through research and my own inner 'channelling' I have discovered many new ideas and techniques.

The Mystical Crystal is a much expanded and updated version of *The Healing Crystal*. It is your crystal reference book, your crystal resource book and I have tried to keep it as simple and straightforward as possible.

One of the nicest compliments that people paid me after my first book appeared was when complete strangers telephoned and told me that they had found my book very easy to follow and understand. Some even said that their lives had been completely changed from reading my book.

There are hundreds of books on the subject of crystals and crystal healing and many of them even I have great difficulty in understanding.

I cannot stress enough that I do not possess the monopoly of ideas and knowledge about crystal healing. I learn something new each day, and I hope I shall continue to do so. But I am always happy to share my experiences and thoughts with as many people as possible and if you wish to write to me for help or advice I will be privileged to hear from you.

So read on – and I hope you find whatever it is you seek; the exciting world of crystals lies before you.

Geoffrey Keyte

UK address
Geoffrey Keyte
37 Bromley Road
St Annes-on-Sea
Lancashire
FY8 1PQ
England

US address
Geoffrey Keyte
The Mystical Crystal
217 Park Avenue
Box 332
Worcester
MA 01609-2243, USA

Email: 100347.2724@compuserve.com

World Wide Web:-
http://www.nitehawk.com/Mystical.Crystal/

Chapter 1

Choosing, Cleansing and Dedicating Crystals

Choosing your crystals

All crystals and gemstones 'vibrate' on their own individual frequency. In that respect they are similar to human beings. We have all had the experience of meeting a stranger for the first time and either liking the person immediately or feeling an inexplicable antipathy towards him, yet quite unable to explain our feelings or emotions.

To fall in love is a beautiful and wondrous experience – the coming together of two minds, two spirits and two physical bodies, both 'vibrating' on the same frequency. Crystals and gemstones should be chosen in exactly the same way. It is very important that the stones we choose and use should 'vibrate' on a frequency as close as possible to our own.

Individual methods of choosing crystals and gemstones vary from person to person but normally include the following:

1) Close your eyes and quietly meditate for a few

moments. Then open your eyes very quickly and pick up the very first stone to which your eye becomes naturally drawn.

2) Run your hand over all the stones available for selection. You will discover that one stone will 'stick' to your hand as if it is 'tacky' or surrounded with glue. This is your stone.

3) You will instinctively 'know' which stone you should choose and which one is right for you. You might sense a strong crystalline white light radiating from the stone and attracting you like a magnet.

4) If you are a competent dowser you should be able to select the most appropriate stone by using your own dowsing techniques. And sometimes you truly feel as if your stones are actually choosing you! This has often happened to me. My most powerful and energised quartz crystals have all arrived on my doorstep for a particular purpose with a special reason for wanting me to work with them. Usually they have been either free or cost very little money.

To choose a quartz crystal or gemstone for a friend, follow exactly the same principles as if you were choosing a stone for yourself but visualise your friend, as strongly as possible, within your mind's eye. With a little practice you will soon find that it is very easy to select just the right crystal or gemstone for any of your friends.

Although more and more retail outlets are now selling crystals and gemstones there are still many places in the United Kingdom where it is extremely difficult to purchase crystals and stones in person.

For many people, the only real opportunity they have to select a crystal or gemstone personally is to attend one of the regular workshops and seminars that I run under the auspices of Crystal 2000. At these workshops and seminars there are always a large selection of crystals, gem-stones and books available for purchase.

However, there are many people, throughout the United Kingdom, who are unable to participate in any of these workshops and seminars and who rely on my personal intuition to select the most appropriate crystal or gemstone on their behalf. In such cases I find that I am either able to work on their name 'vibration' alone or on the 'vibrations' emanating from their original letter. From the feedback I receive it would appear that this method works extremely well in most cases.

Cleansing your crystals

Having chosen your crystal or gemstone it is very important that you 'cleanse' it. Quartz crystals and gemstones easily attract all kinds of 'vibrations'; negative as well as positive. The stones are always 'open' to receiving impressions from everyone and everything around them.

The stone you have selected may well have travelled many thousands of miles before reaching you – and may also have acquired many negative energies and 'vibrations' in its long journey to find you!

Therefore before starting to use your stone in any way it is important that you remove any of these negative 'vibrations' and discordant energies before you start to use your stone. You must do everything you can to ensure that only the most natural and purest energies remain within your stone.

The cleansing method which you use is a matter of personal choice, sometimes dependent upon the amount of time you have available, but I strongly recommend that you use one of the following methods all of which I have found to be very successful:

1) Hold your stone in either your left or right hand and say these words, 'I will and command that this stone be self-cleansing'. As you repeat these words, either out loud or in your head, you should visualise the negative energies falling away from the stone and only the natural, pure energies remaining.

2) Hold your stone under cold or tepid, but never hot, flowing water from the tap. Again, visualise all the negative energies and 'vibrations' being washed away and only the natural, pure energies remaining. When drying your stone after cleansing in water never use a towel or cloth. Always allow your stone to dry naturally – preferably from the rays of the sun. The sun is a powerful energiser and should be used whenever possible.

If, however, there is little or no sun around then allow your stone to dry as naturally as possible in the warmth within your home.

3) Immerse your stone in salt water for several hours. Dry as in (2) above.

4) Bury the stone under the earth in your garden. Our planet consists of at least one third quartz and the powerful magnetic energy field found in the earth will cleanse your stone of all its negativity very effectively.

N.B. If you own a dog – be very careful! Dogs find it great fun to dig up crystals.

5) Place your stone on a large quartz crystal cluster for a few hours. The strong crystalline energies present within the cluster will soon neutralise any negative energies within your stone.

Dedicating your crystals

As all quartz crystals and gemstones respond instantly to the 'intent of will' of the person using them, there is always the strong possibility that crystalline energy may be misused, abused or misdirected.

According to Edgar Cayce, the great American seer, the downfall of Atlantis – and its eventual destruction – was caused by the gross misuse, by certain evil priests who sought only eternal power, of all the sacred knowledge and energies.

These corrupt men experimented by 'inter-breeding' incompatible sources of energy and power. This resulted in the creation of new vibrational frequencies that they were able to place under their personal control. These new vibrations were then implanted within the cells of other living creatures, which led to terrible physical and mental deformities.

The offspring of many of these deformed creatures feature in myths and legends that still persist today. Monsters, some half-man, half-beast; demons; giants; all appear to have been let loose throughout the world for thousands of years. In the end they all had to be spiritually destroyed before they could upset the vibrational balances within the energies of Mother Earth.

We can see, therefore, that in the wrong hands crystalline energy may be used for evil or negative purposes and it is up to all of us to protect our personal quartz crystals and gemstones from all such abuse.

Crystals always attract inquisitive minds and hands and many of these hands transmit negative or unhappy 'vibrations' which your crystal can easily pick up.

To protect your crystals and gemstones from all

potentially harmful energies and 'vibrations', hold your stone in your hand and say the following words. 'I will and command that this stone be used only for the highest benefit of myself and the people with whom I shall be working'.

Your stone has now been 'cleansed' and 'dedicated' and is ready for 'programming'.

CHAPTER 2

Programming your Crystals

All quartz crystals and gemstones will respond to the 'intent' of your own will, whether in word or thought. By simply wishing – or visualising – the crystalline energy to be used in a particular way, it will be! It really is that simple.

Quartz crystals are usually 'programmed' for the following purposes:

    a) Meditation
    b) Healing
    c) Absent healing
    d) Manifesting

a) Meditation

Throughout the world, every minute of the day, countless people practise their own form of meditation. Every person finds solace and comfort in their own particular way.

By holding a quartz crystal or an amethyst in your hand while participating in whichever type of meditation is appropriate to your needs, you will enhance and enrich the spiritual depths of your own meditative experience. The quartz crystal or amethyst enables you to undertake a new and wondrous journey within the inner recesses of your soul. Previously uncharted pathways will open up before you. A new dimension of self-expression will rise to the surface and expand your inner consciousness and awareness.

The amethyst is well known for its ability to relieve mental and physical stress and tension. It is the stone that contains inner peace and tranquillity; the stone of sublime relaxation.

Every member of your meditation circle or group should have their own piece of quartz crystal or amethyst to hold throughout the meditation session. As time passes, perhaps slowly at first, each person will gradually notice that their breathing has become far deeper and more rhythmical and they will have entered a completely new world of inner peace and harmony.

All meditation rooms benefit greatly from having large quartz crystals placed at all four corners of the room, with their single-terminated points directed towards the centre of the room. The crystals should be placed either on the floor or affixed to the corners of the ceiling.

Each of the four quartz crystals in the meditation room should be 'programmed' to project gentle, loving, relaxing energy towards all those in the meditation group. The crystals will then generate a field of positive crystalline energy surrounding everyone in the room.

As well as each member of the group holding their own amethyst or quartz crystal, a large amethyst or quartz crystal cluster may be placed in the middle of the group. This cluster should then be 'programmed' to release beautiful cosmic crystalline energies into every corner of the room.

It is important that one member of the meditation group is nominated to look after the group's amethyst or quartz crystal cluster, and to make absolutely certain that it is properly 'cleansed', 'dedicated' and 'programmed'.

If you hold your crystal or amethyst when meditating with music you will often discover that some quite amazing effects are produced. Occasionally you might even be able to 'see' the music in terms of colour and shape. Even if you are just listening to a piece of music while holding your stone, and not consciously trying to meditate, you will find the depth of experience greatly enriched by the presence of your crystal or amethyst.

Whenever harmonious music is being played in the presence of your crystal or amethyst, the mood and thoughts of the composer become deeply embedded within the very heart of the crystal and if you 'listen' to the crystal afterwards, with your inner ear, you will often be able to pick up the esoteric meaning of the music itself.

You can use your crystal or amethyst in many ways when meditating. Do not be afraid to experiment and try new methods. Listen to what your crystal is saying and try to respond accordingly. You will find the results truly amazing and very worth while.

b) Healing

Once you have chosen your quartz crystal and 'cleansed' and 'dedicated' it, you are ready to start using it for healing purposes.

It is very important that, for the best results your crystal should only be used for either healing or meditation, not for both. The 'vibrations' and 'energies' used in healing and meditation are very different and to use the same crystal in both cases would result in the dissipation of the crystal's unique energies.

Quartz crystals are only 'tools'. By themselves they are inanimate but when they become activated by the human mind they can become extremely powerful indeed.

All human beings possess an inherent healing energy but in most people this healing ability remains dormant. However, when we learn how to channel our own healing energy through our quartz crystals we can then amplify this healing power and the resultant crystal energy can be used for many positive healing purposes.

You may not wish to become a qualified crystal healing therapist yourself but there are still plenty of opportunities for you to use your quartz crystal to heal your family and friends.

I returned home one day from a crystal healing work-shop to discover that my youngest child, Cameron, who was only a few months old, was very ill. My wife had taken him to our local doctor who had told her that if he did not improve within the next couple of days he would have to go into hospital. I felt that I had to do something. When Cameron was ready for bed that evening I cradled him in my arms and placed an electro-crystal therapy wand on his stomach. I also held my personal healing quartz crystal and directed its energy to completely envelop Cameron's body. I gave him crystal healing for only 30 minutes, at the end of which, little Cameron was fast asleep. The next morning, he was almost completely cured and there was no need for Judith to take him back to the doctor or for him to go into hospital.

When treating a patient the following guidelines may prove helpful:

At the beginning of the healing session hold your

quartz crystal in whichever hand feels most comfortable and calmly attune yourself to the inner energies of your quartz crystal. You will probably experience energies 'throbbing' within your hand.

Next, direct the single-terminated end of your healing crystal towards your patient and gently move the crystal around the perimeter of their body in a clockwise direction. As you do this, visualise a blue-white crystalline light emanating from the apex of the crystal, flowing towards and surrounding the patient. Do this several times and it will help to strengthen the electro-magnetic field of energy that surrounds the patient.

The single-terminated end of the quartz crystal should then be directed towards whichever part of the patient's body you believe or sense to be most in need of healing. Once again visualise, as strongly as possible, a lovely blue-white light emanating from the apex of your crystal. Direct this light, like a laser beam, to that part of the patient's body where you feel that healing is most needed. This lovely blue-white light will become stronger and brighter, and the energy between the crystal and your patient will gradually begin to intensify.

The healing session can last as long as you like, and you will know instinctively when the time is right to bring it to an end. To finish the treatment session you should visualise the blue-white light gently flowing back into your quartz crystal. Once more you should direct and project the healing energies in a clockwise direction around your patient's body. Then allow your patient to relax for a few minutes.

Many of my patients fall asleep during treatment sessions so it is very important that you bring them back to the present in as relaxed a manner as possible.

Meditation with quartz crystal (see page 20)

It is best if your patient does not have to drive for a while after the crystal healing session as the patient often becomes so de-stressed and almost 'spaced out' that it can take a while to become re-oriented.

While I quite often do discuss a patient's medical history with them before offering any form of treatment, I have found that it is not always necessary to know in advance what is medically wrong with my patient.

A lady whom I once visited in London was keen for me to demonstrate some of my crystal healing techniques on her. I duly obliged by first directing some crystalline healing energy towards her third eye chakra. Immediately she told me that she had felt the crystal healing energy 'hit' her third eye and then travel down through her body and into her stomach. It later transpired that she had undergone a serious stomach operation a couple of weeks previously and, naturally, that was the part of her body which most needed the crystal healing energies.

I personally believe that all dis-ease occurs purely as a result of an imbalance of our normal bodily 'vibrations'. Therefore, whatever health condition we may be suffering from, whether it be cancer or simply a common cold, the basic treatment remains much the same. The only basic necessity is for the disharmonious or imbalanced 'vibrations' to be re-harmonised, re-energised and re-balanced. This may appear to be an over-simplification but years of experience has shown me that all too often we can over-complicate our diagnoses.

The main difference between allopathic medicine and natural medicine is that allopathic medicine treats symptoms whereas natural medicine concentrates on finding the root cause of the health problem.

Once we discover the originating cause or 'imbalance' of any health condition or disease then, by using crystal healing techniques to rebalance the 'vibrations' which are out of alignment, we can effect a cure or, at the very least, a gradual improvement in the patient's overall health.

You may also use your quartz crystal for self-healing. All you have to do is direct the single-terminated end of your crystal towards the appropriate part of your own body and, as before, visualise a blue-white light radiating from the apex of your crystal, like a laser beam, into your own body.

Crystal healing is one of the most powerful and successful methods of re-balancing, re-energising and re-harmonising every part of the physical and mental bodies.

c) Absent – or Distant – Healing

Quartz crystals are often used very successfully in all forms of absent – or distant – healing. Whether you are three miles, or 3,000 miles away from your patient, crystal healing can prove most effective. For best results the quartz crystals which you use for absent healing should be kept solely for that purpose. It is only necessary for me to have the name of the person who wishes to receive absent healing as, using the unique power of quartz crystals, absent healing can work solely on the name 'vibration'.

All you have to do is visualise the crystalline energy pulsating within the healing crystal being projected towards your patient, wherever they may live. Your quartz crystal will do the rest. If you possess a photograph of your patient or, if you have met him and know what he looks like, just hold your crystal in your hands and visualise, as strongly as possible, the crystalline energy totally surrounding the patient.

After the absent healing session has been completed it is very helpful if you place your crystal on a photograph of your patient. This assists the amplification of the crystalline energy which is being projected by the crystal towards your patient.

In my own healing centre I use a Master absent healing quartz crystal for all my absent healing treatments. Whenever I am asked for absent healing I inscribe the patient's name and relevant details in my absent healing book. I then place my Master absent healing quartz crystal on top of this book with the 'programme' that every name entered in the book will receive healing from the crystalline energies, each according to his or her needs.

I ask that everyone tries to link up with my Master absent healing quartz crystal at 10pm every evening. Those of you reading these words who need my crystal healing, prayers, powers and energies, please try to sit quietly by yourself at 10pm each evening; relax and visualise the crystalline energies flowing into your crown chakra. Think of me and you will receive crystal healing energy from the divine crystalline source.

d) Manifesting

Very simply, manifesting is a method of 'programming' your quartz crystal to help your subconscious mind create something tangible in your life that you may need. Notice that I use the word 'need' not 'want'. There is a big difference! Before you proceed with any form of manifesting it is important that you examine your conscience and decide exactly what you wish to achieve. Decide, in as much detail as possible, what it is you need to acquire.

To avoid dissipating the crystalline energies, it is

essential that you use your chosen crystal for manifesting purposes only.

Remember, need not want, should be your main criterion. We might all say that we want to win a million on the football pools but that is definitely a want – not a need!

Make yourself comfortable in an easy chair and let us start to manifest your innermost needs.

First, hold your quartz crystal in front of you, with both hands. Stare at it intently and visualise yourself entering into the crystal through a door cut into the crystal. Once through this door you will find yourself in a long narrow hall. At the end of this hall is a green door inscribed with the words 'Manifesting Room' upon it.

Open the door of this manifesting room, step inside and look around. The walls are solid gold; the floor is green; the ceiling is studded with millions of precious gemstones, sparkling with all the colours of the rainbow. The room is filled with a warm, rich feeling of prosperity. Bring into your mind a complete and exact image of whatever it is you wish to manifest. Visualise as much detail as possible; concentrate as hard as you can and imagine that you actually possess whatever it is you are manifesting. You are extremely happy and relaxed, secure in the knowledge that your need has been met. Take as long as you like and, when you have finished, slowly walk back out of the manifesting room, closing the door firmly behind you. Walk back along the hall and step outside of the crystal. Take a deep breath, relax your body and when you feel comfortable, open your eyes.

Do your manifesting at least twice a day (morning and evening) until your need has been fulfilled.

CHAPTER 3

The Healing Properties
of Gemstones

Although, obviously, there can never be any guarantee of
a permanent cure or even improvement, there have been
many occasions when the stones referred to in this chapter
have helped to bring about a positive improvement in many
different diseases and health conditions.

As the former director of The Crystal Research
Foundation and current director of Crystal 2000, over the
years I have been responsible for sending out hundreds
of gemstones, mostly in the form of pendants, to people
throughout the country. From some of the letters I have
received I know that many of these gemstones have had a
positive effect upon the recipients.

From both personal experience and talking to other
people who have successfully received healing from their
gemstones, I have found that the most effective way to use
any gemstone for healing purposes is to wear it as close to
the skin as possible. Some ladies tuck their gemstones inside
their bras but most people prefer to wear their chosen

gemstone around their neck on a silver- or gold-plated chain. As well as enabling the healing energies of the gemstone to penetrate the subtle body more easily, the gemstone pendant is a beautiful piece of jewellery.

Gemstones may be held in the hand while watching television or while reading a book or magazine. You can also place your gemstone under your pillow at night while you sleep, thus allowing the energies of the stone to gently penetrate your subtle body throughout the night.

The healing and therapeutic power of crystals and gemstones has even reached boardroom level. At recent natural health exhibitions, for example, I have sold large amethyst clusters to company directors to place on their office desks or in their boardroom. It appears that amethyst or quartz crystal clusters are the current executive toy!

Certain stones can help you to develop your spiritual abilities and gifts. Use amethyst for developing your intuitive awareness; lapis lazuli for acquiring wisdom and truth; moonstone for obtaining humanitarian love and sensitivity. Use gemstones wisely in the pursuit of your ambitions and needs.

However, be aware that your gemstones can never become miracle workers. They need loving care and attention, and your mental attunement with their unique properties and energies, before they can truly help you.

In my first book, *The Healing Crystal*, I included 72 gemstones within this chapter. However, since writing that book my research and experience have increased my knowledge and understanding. I have, therefore, added a considerable number of stones to the original list.

Abalone

A stone for strengthening the muscular tissue, especially around the heart. Very good in the treatment of spinal degenerative diseases.

Agate

Semi-precious stone, said to improve natural vitality and energy and to increase the self-confidence of the wearer. It is believed to be especially beneficial to athletes and those taking any kind of examination or test, or anyone who has to call upon sudden bursts of mental or physical energy. Agate balances the emotions and calms the body, mind and feelings. Aids general healing, reduces fever, hardens tender gums, gives courage and banishes fear. Helps to develop powers of eloquence. Stone of health and good fortune.

Albite

Strengthens the lungs, spleen and thymus.

Alexandrite

Helps the nervous system, spleen, pancreas and testicles. May be used to amplify colour therapy.

Amazonite

Generally used to help soothe the nervous system and to give relief to those suffering from emotional disturbances. Also helps with metabolism and growth. Useful when trying to express oneself more clearly. Regulates and improves thinking abilities.

Amber

Not really a stone but the yellow-brown fossilised resin of trees. Used to best effect by those suffering from throat infections, bronchial disorders or those prone to asthma or convulsions. Also useful for rheumatism, intestinal disorders, earache, bladder trouble, nerves or bone-marrow deficiencies. Calming, can absorb negative energy and help the body to heal itself. Used for making and breaking spells. Helps lift depression and suicidal tendencies.

Amethyst

A purple-coloured quartz used as a semi-precious stone, the amethyst is known as a spiritual stone and is used for general healing and meditation. It is said that sleeping with a piece of amethyst beneath one's pillow promotes intuitive dreams and inspired thought. Many healers consider it useful for the relief of insomnia and to bring solace in times of grief. Amethyst clears, purifies and helps with addictions, stress or tension. It also protects against blood disease, the toxic effects of substance use, acne, neuralgia and fits. Soothes and calms the mind, raises the spirit, re-balances and increases intuitive awareness, protects from negative vibrations. Traditionally believed to protect from drunkenness.

Anhydrite

Strengthens the kidneys and ovaries.

Apache Tear

Used in 'grounding' one's energies; also helps soul reflection.

Apatite

Strengthens muscle tissue, helps in co-ordinating basic motor responses. Helps those who suffer from stuttering and is also used in the treatment of hypertension.

Aqua-Aura

Improves heart, lungs, throat, and thymus. Good for those suffering from emotional trauma. Aids release of inner emotional tension from deep within the body. Helps meditation.

Aquamarine

A bluish-green transparent beryl, the aquamarine is believed to be most useful when dealing with problems of the eyes, liver, throat, stomach, nerves, and glands. Relieves toothache, improves sight. Preserves innocence. Quickens intellect, increases self-knowledge. It is also reputed to promote clear and logical thinking and for that reason is often carried as a 'good luck' charm by those taking examinations or being interviewed for a job. Brings inspiration and new ideas.

Atacamite

Strengthens the genitals, thyroid and the nervous system. Used in the treatment of venereal diseases, including herpes.

Auricalcite

Similar to smithsonite.

Aventurine

Said to be useful in relieving migraine and in soothing the eyes. A traditional method of using this stone is to leave it in water overnight and bathe the eyes in the water the following day. Aventurine water can also be used for bathing irritations of the skin. Aventurine is a soother and helps relax one for a better night's sleep. It also relieves tension and shock. Improves vitality, equalises blood pressure. Encourages creativity, gives the wearer courage, independence and serenity.

Azurite

A natural blue copper carbonate, said to be an aid to psychic development, azurite is a very powerful stone. It aids meditation and has the ability to penetrate your deepest subconscious fears. Used as a general healing stone it also relieves arthritis, joint disabilities and reduces hip joint pain.

Beryl

Helps with heart problems, liver trouble, mouth, stomach and throat infections. Improves intellect, strengthens willpower, guards against stupidity and mental disorders.

Bloodstone

A deep-green precious stone flecked with red, bloodstone is believed to help overcome depression and melancholia – especially when worn by the sufferer. It is also said to help those who suffer from psychosomatic illness and pains which have an emotional rather than a physical cause.

Bloodstone purifies the blood and detoxifies the organs, particularly the liver, kidneys and spleen. It helps to allow light into the body. Provides vitality, strengthens idealism and the will to do good. Increases one's talent, stimulates the kundalini and balances all of the chakras.

Blue-lace Agate

Blue-lace agate is a very calming stone helpful for freely expressing oneself. Provides cool and soothing energy which is good for neutralising red energies such as anger, infections, inflammations, fevers etc. Helps to open the throat chakra.

Blue Quartz

Helps improve heart, lungs, throat and thymus. Good for people suffering from emotional trauma. Aids the release of inner emotional tension from deep within the body.

Boji Stone

Has general healing qualities and assists tissue regeneration. Strengthens all the chakras and meridians.

Calcite (gold)

Carries the golden healing ray. Gives comfort, helps lift depression. Good for most ailments.

Calcite (green)

Helps the kidneys, spleen and pancreas. Removes toxins from the body and alleviates mental fear. Aids mental clarity, soothes anxiety, calms turbulent energies. Expands awareness, aids intuition, links parallel realities. Good when undertaking mental change.

Calcite (orange)

Helps the gall bladder, improves physical energy and expands awareness.

Calcite (optical)
Improves eyesight. Brings spiritual understanding into challenging circumstances and situations. Helps when doing regression.

Carnelian
Semi-precious stone, a reddish variety of chalcedony.

Useful for understanding one's rhythms and cycles and it is said that if worn in a pouch around the neck by women during menstruation carnelian will help to ease stomach cramps.

Strengthens voice. Helps rheumatism and arthritis, depression, neuralgia. Aids the sense of touch. Used for infertility and impotence. Alleviates blood poisoning, fever, infection and nose bleeds. Helps in the treatment of sores, spasms and wounds. Protects from evil, elevates the spirit, grounds energies thus assisting concentration by clearing the mind and focusing one's thoughts. Helps daydreamers and those who are absent-minded.

Celestite
Helps to ease tension, opens the mind and develops awareness. Cools the overactive mind, helps to relax muscles. Elevates consciousness. Promotes peaceful co-existence and harmonious interaction with other aspects of creation.

Chalcedony
Improves bone-marrow, spleen, red corpuscles and heart tissue. Stimulates optimism and enhances spiritual and artistic creativity.

Chalcopyrite (peacock)
Helps cheer those with constant worries. Also improves prosperity consciousness.

Charoite
Dissolves fear including the fear of fear itself! Will help the fear rise to the surface so that it may be faced and dealt with.

Chrysocolla
Relieves nervous tension, emotional congestion, ulcer or stomach problems. Brings balance, cleanses all negativity, brings inner peace and contentment.

Chrysolite
Strengthens the appendix. Alleviates general toxaemia and viral conditions.

Chrysoprase
Improves prostate gland, testicles, fallopian tubes and ovaries. Increases fertility.

Citrine
Yellow variety of quartz, claims to give a sense of direction to those who feel they have lost their path in life.

Helps to control the emotions and works with relationships and self-knowledge. Attracts self-worth, dissolves emotional blocks and induces dreams. Also said to be beneficial to people suffering from poor circulation. Strengthens the immune system; aids tissue regeneration. Eases toxic conditions particularly in the endocrine and digestive systems. Helps with diabetes and depression.

Activates mental powers and clarifies thought. Improves self-image bringing confidence into relationships and environment, improving the quality of one's life, sometimes bringing prosperity. Reduces harmful effect of electrical products.

Conicalcite
Cheering stone, helpful with symbolic re-birth, helps strengthen new resolutions.

Coral
Hard substance formed of skeletons of various marine polyps. Said to promote general physical and mental well-being and to help in particular those suffering from anaemia, bladder conditions, colic and whooping cough.

In many parts of the world it is believed that coral can be used to ward off evil thoughts sent by ill-wishers.

Crocidolite
Used to help those who become over-preoccupied with their own personal limitations.

Diamond
Master healer. An extremely powerful stone used for the removal of blockages and all emotional negativity.

Dioptase
An emerald green silicate of copper. A general healer which relieves mental stress, promotes abundance, relaxation, love and emotional expressiveness.

Heals the parts emotionally abandoned while experiencing heartache. Good for those who, through loss, fear to love again, helps heal the heart and helps one to be able to trust again.

Dolomite
Used to help those who lack resourcefulness and who have an acute fear of personal failure.

Emerald
Bright green precious stone that improves intellect and memory. Helps tired eyes and insomnia. Improves eloquence. Gives power to see into the future and grants success in business. Acts as an emotional stabiliser. Said to help release emotionally-based trauma. Opens up the heart to love, peace and healing.

Fluorite
Helps bring the spiritual into the material and quickens enlightenment. Helps heal holes in one's aura where energy is drained. Grounds, balances and focuses one's energies. Absorbs and alters negative and other energies. Opens the chakras. Aids physical and mental healing. Strengthens bone tissue, especially tooth enamel. Relieves dental disease, pneumonia, viral inflammation.

Galena
Strengthens lungs, thyroid, and the nervous system. Protects against depression and skin diseases. Promotes self-confidence, pride and success. Improves imagination.

Garnet
Most frequently used as a general tonic for the whole system – physical, mental and emotional. It is regenerative and

revitalising, strengthens the blood and helps with anaemia and circulatory problems.

Protects against infection, depression and skin diseases. Brings into consciousness the physical powers and is particularly recommended for those who need to improve their self-respect and self-confidence and to increase courage when dealing with changes.

Improves imagination. Assists in dreamwork and in past life recall. Increases determination, energy and courage. Attracts love, promotes bonding.

Gem Silica – Chrysoprase

Apple green variety of chalcedony. Reveals will-power and is useful for dealing with depression and loss of incentive.

Feminine stone, ideal for menstrual pain and premenstrual tension. Helps after miscarriages, abortions, hysterectomies. Helps with birthing if held, worn or meditated upon during labour.

Cools fevers, heals burns, calms nerves, helps thyroid imbalance, voice problems, neck/shoulder strain. Develops patience, kindness, tolerance, compassion, humility. Gives peace and serenity, emotional balance; eases sorrow and anger. Good for men who, traditionally, find it difficult to express their feelings or emotions.

Excellent stone for meditation and can assist the development of clairvoyance.

Grossuralite

Used in the treatment of people who fear emotional hostility from everyone surrounding them.

Hematite

A natural ferric oxide, hematite improves all blood disorders. Reduces stressful effects of air travel, combats insomnia. Enhances astral projection, promotes balance, focus, convergence and concentration of energy. Said to increase courage. Also claimed to strengthen the heart and is good for reducing a rapid pulse.

Herderite

This stone stimulates the pancreas and spleen and helps to restore the balance in erratic emotional behaviour.

Herkimer Diamond

Releases stress and tension throughout the body, boosts the power of other crystals by being used to close the circuit, particularly effective with boji stones.

Howlite (magnetite)

A natural sulphide or iron. Aids digestive system of abdomen and upper intestinal tract. Eases anxiety, depression, frustration and false hopes.

Strengthens astral body. Opens mind to new ideas, intellectually stimulating, links left and right hemispheres of brain facilitating communication between logic and emotion. Promotes powers of analysis and creativity, psychic development, memory, channelling activities, strength of will.

Iron Pyrite

Pyrite is claimed to increase the oxygen supply in the blood, to strengthen the circulatory system in general and to be useful in clearing congested air passages.

Ivory
Protects the physical body from injury.

Jacinth
Promotes spiritual sight and understanding. Used in childbirth. Helps in the treatment of insomnia.

Jade
A pale green gemstone said to help in relieving kidney complaints, bladder trouble and eye problems.

Yellow jade is believed to aid a poor digestion. When worn as a piece of jewellery, jade is thought to provide protection from one's enemies and can be used for protection on long journeys.

Also used to attract good luck, for wisdom, for long life and a peaceful death. Helps to control dream content. In ancient China and Egypt it was widely used as a talisman to attract good fortune, friendship and loyalty.

Jasper
Coloured impure form of natural silica said to be both invigorating and stabilising, bringing stillness to a troubled mind. Generates an even rhythmic pulse and is also said to improve the sense of smell and to overcome depression.

Red jasper is known to contain iron oxide which is used medically to control excessive bleeding. It is claimed, therefore, that it can be useful in overcoming disorders of the blood. Also used for digestion and stomach problems, biliousness and bladder trouble. Protects from witchcraft, soothes the nerves.

Jet
A very hard lustrous form of natural carbon. Prevents deep depression, quietens fears. Protects from violence and illness. Aids grieving. Also used in healing to control and ease migraine and pain behind the eyes.

Kunzite
Alleviates anaemia, improves general tissue rejuvenation. Creates balance between heart and mind, clears emotional blockages. In meditation can balance negative emotional and troubled mental states.

Kyanite
Used in meridian points to stimulate flow of energy, or on chakra centres to clear blockages. Recalls past lives when placed on third eye. Augments channelling, altered states, vivid dreams, clear visualisation, loyalty, honour and serenity.

Kyanite blades can make incisions in the auric field. Can also cut through layers of mental misconceptions and create new lines of energy for new thought.

Lapis Lazuli
A brilliant blue mineral, the lapis lazuli was called the Stone of Heaven by the ancient Egyptians and is thought by many to be the stone upon which were carved the laws given to Moses.

It is said to prevent fits and epilepsy and to improve the eyesight. Helps heart and spleen; protects against strokes; helps lift depression. Also helps with the acquisition of wisdom and truth.

A symbol of power and a mental and spiritual

cleanser. Assists psychic development and mental stability. Gives hope and self-awareness and helps one to face one's shadow-self. The stone of friendship. Helps cut through superficialities to find inner truth. Aura cleanser.

Larimar
Soothes sore throats and tonsillitis. Helps express new ideas. Brings harmony between heart and mind. Good for schizophrenics. Transmutes anger, greed, frustration to peace; calms excess energies by re-balancing.

Lazulite
Improves and stimulates the pineal glands and liver.

Lazurite
Stimulates visions and amplifies thought-form. Also used for tissue rejuvenation.

Lepidolite
Unifies mind and heart, heals whatever inhibits this merging. Used in the treatment of schizophrenia.

Lepidolite with Rubellite
Good for introverted, shy people who are unable to express love in external ways.

Luvulite (sugilite)
Restores balance to pineal, pituitary and left and right brain hemispheres. Helps with autism, dyslexia, epilepsy, physical coordination problems, visual problems, spiritual problems.

Magnetite
Stimulates endocrine system. Improves blood circulation. Helps in meditation.

Malachite
A green copper carbonate, malachite contains copper and is claimed to be helpful in the treatment of rheumatism and also in regularising menstruation. Used also in the treatment of asthma and toothache. Improves eyesight.

Raises one's spirits and increases hope, health and happiness. Attracts physical and material benefits and brings prosperity. Assists wise rule and helps remove mental blockages hindering spiritual growth. Relieves any congestion in the body and helps with confusion, a lack of purpose and insecurity.

Marcasite
Gentle physical strengthener. Makes one feel more able to cope with any problems and difficulties.

Mimetite
Helps communication; grounds and insulates.

Moldavite
Small glassy greeny stone believed to be associated with meteorites.

Eases epilepsy, brain imbalances and malfunctions and autism, particularly if brought on by excessive sensitivity.

Assists conscious communication with star-seed sources and is a healing balm for the deep longing of many people to 'go home'. Moldavite also helps one to understand one's true purpose in life. A stone for transformation.

Moonstone

Moonstone is an opalescent feldspar claimed to promote long life and happiness and said to attract friendship and loyalty towards the wearer.

Acts as a mediator between mind and emotions and allows peace of mind and accessibility to one's innerself. Helps soothe and balance emotion.

In healing terms, often used to reduce excess fluid in the body and to reduce any attendant swelling. Used for women suffering from pre-menstrual tension.

Gives inspiration, encourages personal attachments. Helps obtain humanitarian love, romance and sensitivity.

Morganite

Strengthens the larynx, lungs, thyroid and nervous system.

Morion Crystal

A smokey quartz crystal so dark it seems black instead of the more usual brown. Very good for grounding.

Moss-Agate

Said to cleanse the emotional body and release anger and frustration.

Obsidian Snowflake

A grounding stone – makes the user face up to responsibility. Dedicated to change, metamorphosis, purification, fulfilment, inner growth and introspection. Deflects negative energy.

Onyx

A variety of agate, the onyx is reputed to improve concentration and devotion which is perhaps why it is frequently found in rosaries.

Helps hearing problems, heart trouble and ulcers.

Opal

Helps lung conditions, increases assimilation of protein. Assists the control of one's temper and calms the nerves.

Aids the development of psychic ability. Sometimes considered an unlucky stone, perhaps because it causes one's thoughts, good or bad, to rebound.

Above all, it is a stone of love, but if the lover be false its influence is reversed, and the opal proves a sorry stone for faithless lovers.

Pearl

Promotes antibodies and fights infection.

Peridot

Peridot, as well as being recommended as a cure for insomnia, is said to aid the digestion and placate the nervous system.

Improves bruised eyes. Can cleanse and heal hurt feelings, helps mend damaged relationships.

Attracts occult powers to the user. Develops inner vision; the stone of the seer. Counteracts negativity and opens the mind. Acts like a tonic, heals the physical body and can be useful in reducing fever. Also used in treating emotional states such as anger or jealousy.

Petrified Wood

Restores physical energy. Helps hip and back problems. Aids past-life recall.

Quartz Crystal

A natural crystalline silica, the quartz crystal attracts the powers of light and energy and is said to be a powerful general healer and dynamic working tool. It works on all levels – strengthening, cleansing and protecting.

Purifies the air. Protects against harmful electrical vibrations.

Assists the wearer to think intuitively. Amplifies and transmits subtle vibrations.

The symbol of elemental wholeness, containing the four elements of creation. Assists the development and integration of one's entire being. Helps one to amplify, focus, direct, transmit and store energy.

Its use as an aid to opening the psychic centres, enabling meditation at a deeper level and the liberation of one's mind from the mundane and the trivial, is considered to be its greatest attribute. Quartz crystal releases the higher consciousness and develops mystical and spiritual gifts.

Rhodochrosite

Prevents mental breakdowns, balances physical and emotional traumas. Improves eyesight, kidney, pancreas and spleen. Inspires forgiveness, heals emotional scars, attracts love. Helps one face reality and new situations. Assists integration of physical, mental and emotional fields.

Rhodonite

Restores physical energy, especially following trauma or shock. Strengthens inner ear and improves sense of hearing. Aids vitamin absorption. Increases language skills, raises self-esteem. Helps maintain loving state in everyday life by bolstering one's resolve not to give in without having to be aggressive.

Rhyolite

Rejuvenates physical beauty. Helps increase self-expression and the ability to speak with greater clarity.

Rock Crystal

Relieves diarrhoea, dizziness, haemorrhage, kidney troubles, spasms, vertigo. Helps ease pain anywhere.

Rose Quartz

Claimed to be one of the best stones to use in the treatment of migraines and headaches of all types. Calms emotions, helps suffering due to emotional trauma, heals wounds of neglect. Also said to stimulate the imagination and intellect and to open up the heart to inner peace, self-love and self-recognition. A very healing stone for internal wounds, bitterness and sorrows, it promotes forgiveness, love and friendship. Makes one more receptive to beauty, hastens recovery and gladdens the heart. The Venus or love stone.

Ruby

A deep red transparent gemstone, a form of corundum. As well as aiding intuitive thinking, the ruby is believed to increase levels of energy and divine creativity.

Often used to alleviate disorders of the blood, such

as anaemia, poor circulation and menstrual problems. Also used in the treatment of rheumatism and arthritis. Improves fever, pain and spasms. Alleviates worries, lifts spirits, improves confidence, intuition, spiritual wisdom, energy and courage.

Encourages self-nurturing in those with a poor self-image.

Rutilated Quartz

Rutilated quartz is said to be of particular benefit to those who suffer from respiratory complaints such as asthma, bronchitis etc.

Increases tissue regeneration. Rebalances different levels of consciousness. Improves decisiveness, strengthens one's will.

Sapphire

Helps control of bleeding, insomnia and nervousness. Stone of friendship and love, attracts good influences. Gives the wearer devotion, faith, imagination and peace of mind.

Sardonyx

Stimulates self-control and protection.

Selenite

One of the most powerful healing stones, selenite calms and clears troubled minds and is useful in personal meditation and visualisation.

Stabilises the emotions, bringing them under control. Helps to clarify one's innermost thoughts and to expand one's mental powers.

Used in past-life recall and in regression therapy.

Can be used in any healing treatment but should only be used by a qualified crystal healing therapist who is able to handle and direct the powerful energies property.

Smithsonite

Calms and clears, good to use in high-anxiety situations.

Helps after nervous breakdowns, relaxes over-tense muscles, also good in childbirth. Neutralises red energies.

Smokey Quartz

Disperses negative patterns and vibrations and transmits a high quantity of light. Good luck talisman. Helps protect soldiers on active service.

Improves abdomen, kidneys, pancreas and the sexual organs. Increases energy fertility. Encourages survival instincts. Stimulates and purifies energy centres. Grounds and stabilises energies, helps lift depression. Draws out and absorbs negative energies, replacing them with positive ones.

Snow Quartz

Strengthens immune system. A softer energy than clear quartz.

Used in meditation snow quartz gives serenity and powers of inner contemplation.

Sodalite

A good stone for over-sensitive and defensive people, improves courage and endurance. Balances and stills the mind and clears rigid thought patterns. Helps logical and rational thought, and intellect. Widens the perspective.

Blue sodalite is reputed to assist in lowering of blood pressure and balancing the metabolism. Aids sleep.

Spinel
Attracts help. Makes the wearer strong in character.

Staurolite
Used to help people who suffer from overcaution or doubt.

Sugilite
See luvulite

Thulite
To help those who are resisting a condition or relationship which they regard as discouraging.

Tiger's Eye
Claimed to counteract feelings of hypochondria and the onset of psychosomatic illness. Also gives a feeling of self-confidence.

Especially good for clear thinking and for seeing a problem objectively when confused or emotionally affected. Releases tension and develops will-power.

Good for asthma. Helps one to gain insight into one's own faults. Protects from witchcraft and evil. Attracts good luck.

Topaz (yellow)
A yellowish transparent mineral, topaz helps to overcome stress and soothes nerves thereby helping one to achieve a deeper sleep. Also good for colds and flu. Strengthens blood

vessels, improves blood circulation, varicose veins, sense of taste. Good for liver trouble. Improves the intellect, develops psychic abilities, calms both mind and body.

Topaz (blue)
A calming stone. Good for throat disorders. Inspires leadership ability, psychic insight, spiritual and artistic growth. Helps with clarity and concentration.

Tourmaline (general)
Prevents lymphatic disease. Balances, protects, calms, gives self-confidence and cheerfulness. Attracts inspiration, goodwill and friendship. Protects wearer against misfortune and anaemia. Grounds high-frequency energies into the physicality. Useful for meditation.

Tourmaline (black or green)
Strengthens nervous system, regulates blood pressure. Deflects negative energy, attracts prosperity.

Tourmaline (blue)
Helps with all throat problems, thyroid, speech impediments. Promotes clear verbal expression, dissolves mental friction and emotional constriction.

Tourmaline carries a high electrical charge and if rubbed briskly one end will become positive and the other negative. The resulting energy can be directed wherever peaceful energy is required.

Tourmaline (watermelon/pink)
Heart balancer. Promotes understanding of self and emotions.

Turquoise

A bluish green precious stone, turquoise helps the ability to express oneself and verbalise freely. It is good for laryngitis and nervousness in speech.

It is said that turquoise will grow pale on a sickly person and recover its colour when returned to a healthy person. Can strengthen entire anatomy and helps improve all diseases.

Shields the wearer from harmful influences, attracts friendship. Used in meditation and also for the development of intuition. Brings wisdom and also reminds us of both our spiritual nature and our earthy inheritance and its beauty.

Unakite

Helps balance and gives stability. A grounding stone.

Vanadinite

Helps with throat problems and communication.

Vivianite

Symbol of rebirth, burns away old ways of looking at things and gives one a new perspective on life. Helps clear vision at all levels.

Zircon

General healer. Helps liver complaints, childbirth, insomnia. Promotes spiritual sight and understanding.

Zoisite

Strengthens the male genitals and the female cervix. Helps to increase fertility.

CHAPTER 4

Birthstones

There are twelve signs of the zodiac: Aries, Taurus, Gemini, Cancer, Leo, Virgo, Libra, Scorpio, Sagittarius, Capricorn, Aquarius and Pisces.

I am constantly asked during my workshops and seminars to recommend an appropriate stone for a particular birth sign. In my experience the only accurate way to ascertain the correct birthstone for any individual is for that person to visit a properly qualified astrologist and for a detailed chart to be constructed, based on the person's place of birth, date of birth and the exact time of birth. Any other method is too vague and generalised.

A few years ago, to prove my theory, I studied as many books on the astrological use of gemstones as I could. From all the information available I compiled a comprehensive list – birthsign by birthsign – containing all the recommended birthstones which each book suggested. When my list was complete I discovered that every birthsign had at least nine gemstones which, according to all the books, would be suitable for people born under that

55

particular sign of the zodiac. However, using intuition, logic and a little common-sense, I produced the following chart which serves as a useful guide when I am asked to recommend a particular gemstone for a person's birth sign:

Aries — jasper, ruby
Taurus — rose quartz, lapis lazuli, carnelian, sapphire
Gemini — citrine, rock crystal, tiger's eye, agate, rutile quartz
Cancer — olivine, emerald, moonstone
Leo — quartz crystal, diamond, agate
Virgo — carnelian, agate, jasper, sapphire
Libra — emerald, aventurine, jade, sapphire
Scorpio — garnet, bloodstone, ruby, jasper, beryl
Sagittarius — topaz, jacinth, obsidian snowflake
Capricorn — smokey quartz, ruby, onyx, jet
Aquarius — turquoise, malachite, aquamarine, moonstone
Pisces — amethyst, opal, moonstone

While it is always acceptable to give a friend or loved one a birthstone pendant or necklace, remember that the stones that will work best for you or your friends are the ones whose vibrational energies are most closely compatible with the person who is going to wear it.

CHAPTER 5

'Hands on' Experience with Gemstones

Having read Chapter 3 you now have a working knowledge of the basic energies present within any individual gemstone. There can never, however, be any substitute for experience and it is not until you begin to use crystals and gemstones in your own healing practice and daily life that you can truly begin to understand and appreciate the many wonderful qualities that are to be found within each precious gemstone.

The properties which I have listed as applicable to each gemstone should only be used as a guide. I strongly encourage all of you reading this book to use your own intuitive faculties to discover new ways of using your stones. You may even encounter different properties for the stones which I have not yet discovered myself!

The use of one's own intuitive powers – and the development of inner spiritual sensitivity – is very important at all times when working with crystals and gemstones.

One of my colleagues, Gillian Bull from the Isle of

Man, has been experimenting for some time with many different gemstones and I am indebted to her for allowing me to share some of these experiences with you.

Gillian says:

I have been lucky enough to work with many crystals and gemstones during the past couple of years.

During that time, I have come to know each one well – although not completely, as it is my experience that, even now, they still have several hidden talents hitherto unexpected!

It is always difficult, if impossible, to choose a favourite among so many old friends. Each one rises to the task demanded of it, often giving far more than is ever expected.

Perhaps the fairest way is to comment upon each one and what I, personally, experience when exploring that gemstone whether in a physical or metaphysical context.

Agate

Always a cooling, soothing gem. A solid rock of reassurance and positivity. I find that it grounds me in the reality of the present if I am worrying about future possibilities. I like to carry, touch or wear this gem if I am feeling feverish or on the brink of 'flu. A must in hot, clammy weather.

Agate feels cold to the touch, but is definitely not a cold stone in any other way.

I am drawn particularly to the beautiful grey-banded Botswana agates, so like the fingerprints of the Gods who must once have walked the Earth!

Amazonite

Another cooling gem, and one I particularly value for its feminine associations. It certainly seems to take the sting out of pre-menstrual tension, cools hot flushes and regulates flooding in menopausal ladies. Definitely a balancer of the female psyche during hormonal fluctuations.

I find amazonite has a rather aloof quality that does not seem to invite close contact. I could not wear jewellery made of amazonite for long periods or on a regular basis. Having said that, it is a gem I would never be without, for on a subtle level it seems to radiate common sense and rationality.

Amber

Always warm and vaguely mystical, I find that amber in its clearest form attracts me very much.

Spending a little while holding and exploring amber helps me to make a connection to the essence of the living part of the tree it once was. I can feel the strength and the protection vibrating from it, and it is that, I feel, that gives amber its inbuilt electricity: life itself.

I have not used it widely on a physical level, having only recently acquired some for use in healing. However, in what little experience I have had with it, its potency as a vibrational and penetrating gem cannot be questioned. It is rather like applying deep heat massage to the affected area with, I am told by patients, the same satisfying results.

Amethyst

With the exception of quartz, I use amethyst more than any other crystal. On a physical level, it is a super healer and helps to unlock subconscious blocks that are manifesting as disease.

I find it a wonderful gem to use in stress relief, grief, fears or phobias, confusion and all types of headache.

Amethyst seems to draw the patient beyond the physical manifestation of their problem to the source itself. Once confronted, steps can be taken to eradicate, or at least work through, the underlying cause.

I have seen fantastic results using amethyst in sleep pattern irregularities: in one case twenty years of chronic insomnia was cured within three days, and the patient continues to enjoy deep, unbroken, restful sleep. Interestingly though, her first dream was of a confrontation with her late father. She had never liked him during his life, and felt no emotion whatsoever upon his death. In the dream, she was able to explain to him why she disliked him so much and he, in turn, was able to give her a deeper insight into why he had treated her with such seeming indifference throughout her life. They made their peace with one another and she has never looked back.

I think this is a good example of how amethyst works subtly upon every level, not perhaps with the dynamics of quartz, but with a deeper spiritual insight into every aspect of what makes us what we are. It is impartial and non-judgemental, allowing us to view our own shortcomings with that same quality of detachment.

On a spiritual level, I often use amethyst during meditation and I always have a large amethyst point or cluster in the room during absent healing sessions. Placing a piece upon the brow before and during meditation helps me to connect much more easily to the Higher Self. Images and symbols are vivid, and their subtle meaning is easier to grasp on a conscious level.

For clients just beginning to unfold their higher spiritual potential I recommend amethyst rather than quartz as a starter crystal. I also find that amethyst encourages people who are irresistibly drawn to it to develop their own innate healing abilities, either through crystals or spiritual healing in its varied apsects.

Aventurine

Aventurine feels warm, cheerful and positive, with a somewhat understated power. I find that carrying aventurine around with me boosts my energy levels and encourages a fun approach to life.

On a physical level, I find that aventurine is a very potent healer with the characteristic of 'drawing out' conditions. This aspect should be approached cautiously, as I find that aventurine can work on the emotional level, drawing out old hurts and bitterness, so I usually recommend that it be used in conjunction with rose quartz. This, I find, works well when there is evidence of heart problems or fluctuation in blood pressure levels.

It is a wonderful tonic for strained or tired eyes, and a few moments spent relaxing with a piece of aventurine upon each closed eyelid is soothing and refreshing.

Azurite

Azurite is perhaps the only mineral I have worked with that I feel absolutely no rapport with whatsoever. Sadly, and probably due to my own shortcomings, I feel nothing from this gemstone on any level. It feels neither warm nor cold to the touch, and I get the merest flicker of vibrational energy from it. Meditating upon azurite while holding a piece in my hand, I found it difficult to settle. My thoughts would not be silenced and I could not find the still centre within. After a few moments I developed a headache, and decided to call a halt to the whole thing.

However, I am trying to persevere with azurite because I do feel that, once I have managed to penetrate its frosty exterior, it has a wonderful storehouse of healing and wisdom to be tapped.

Carnelian

What would I do without carnelian? As winter begins to bite and we come into the time of coughs and colds, so too does carnelian come into its own.

Carnelian is like a warm shawl or a comforting hot water bottle, and I use it to treat chest infections, sore throats and irritating coughs with great success. I find it also gives a boost of energy, like a tonic, after colds and 'flu, and restores a positive attitude to life after a debilitating illness. In some respects, I find carnelian to have almost antiseptic qualities, and a piece rubbed on the skin over a scar or wound that is painful and slow to heal works wonders.

I always carry a piece whenever I am asked to give a talk on crystals to various groups, not only because it lends strength to my voice, but because I am chronically shy in such situations, and carnelian gives me the self-confidence and authority I need.

A good friend and an invaluable healing gem!

Garnet

Garnet is a gem that I have not worked with very much, again because I find that I am not drawn to it. On a purely aesthetic level I find its burgundy wine colour beautiful, and quite uplifting. But garnet has a coolness – almost, a stand-offishness – about it that says to me 'look but don't touch'. I find myself a little irritated with garnet's attitude, which I suppose is a manifestation of pride on both parts and which I am actively working to overcome!

Hematite

This is another stone that I would not be without, and I have seen many wonderful healings instigated by hematite. A gentleman suffering from Reynaud's disease was completely cured using hematite.

A lady whose hands were literally frozen into claws due to poor circulation had immediate relief and was able to uncurl her fingers for the first time in years after holding a piece of hematite for just a few moments. She was so astounded and overjoyed to feel warmth and sensation returning to her crippled hand that she became very emotional.

Another lady, aged 89, who I see as part of the Manx Cancer Help programme, sleeps each night clutching her hematite and her quartz, and has just been given a six-month all-clear of breast cancer.

I myself use hematite tucked into my bra to alleviate the discomfort of pre-menstrual mastitis, and swear by its continued success to relieve any lady suffering from the same problem.

I have found that, by restoring, strengthening and augmenting the flow of blood and white cells to a specific area of the body, hematite is capable of almost instantaneous healing and pain relief. It seems to stimulate and multiply natural antibodies in the patient, and aid in the release of endorphins into the bloodstream, immediately triggering the body's own capacity to self-heal.

On a more spiritual level, I find hematite to be a wonderfully grounding stone for use in deep or prolonged meditation. It exudes a sense of safety and complete protection for the body while the mind and spirit are elsewhere. After a fraught or tiring day, hematite held in each hand refreshes, soothes, calms and restores me, helping to clear my mind and preparing me for deep and restful sleep.

Jasper

Jasper is another gem with which I seem to have an on-off relationship! It has a cool feel, but responds quickly to my touch and becomes very warm and soothing.

I have used jasper successfully to treat a young woman who had suffered repeated miscarriages. As soon as she had conceived we began to introduce jasper, and she always had a piece with her throughout the pregnancy. She felt well and very positive throughout her pregnancy, and was eventually delivered of a healthy baby boy.

Jasper is a very feminine gem, and always responds well to any specifically female problem. I have also used it in the treatment of heavy or irregular menstruation, fibroids and painful, tearing menstrual cramps. Even more than moonstone, I consider jasper to be the optimum healer for all uterine and ovarian conditions. Cool and soothing where necessary, warm and comforting as the treatment demands.

A very versatile gem, and one that I have found many women are instinctively drawn to.

Lapis Lazuli

Even as I think of lapis, my hands go to my neck! I don't possess any lapis jewellery through choice, but I find the strong Egyptian influence of lapis, as part of a past life, irresistible.

Unmistakably a noble and holy gem, I have found that lapis attracts mystics and seekers; those who are in the process of retracing the pathways of the past to find relevance to their present day circumstances. Rarely does anyone, in my experience, find themselves drawn to lapis on a purely physical vibration.

I have used it in healing to strengthen back muscles following injury or to help correct poor posture. I also find it to be helpful in cases of headaches that have been brought about by a knock to the head.

Generally, though, I find lapis to be a gem of the intellect, of reason and discernment. A gateway to inner truth and wisdom, and a means to express it once accessed.

Malachite

I use malachite extensively to treat eye problems, asthma and allergies, generally (especially in children) with good results.

One of my clients had an interesting experience with malachite that I think is worth recounting here.

Late one evening he developed a nasty toothache, so decided to place a piece of malachite under his pillow to ease the pain overnight. On a sudden impulse, he placed his quartz point with it to augment malachite's potency, and soon fell fast asleep. That night he relived, in dreams, all the bullying he had suffered during his schooldays in vivid and graphic detail. He awoke drenched in sweat and feeling thoroughly wretched and worn out.

Because he could not get an appointment with the dentist straight away, he passed another night in the same fashion; until it dawned on him that malachite and quartz together were responsible for the dreams that caused him to face, and this time deal with, all his childhood trauma.

Intrigued, he experimented over several nights using just quartz (no problems); just malachite (no problems); and the combination – bingo!

Because he is a very pragmatic and analytical person, he saw this as a chance to confront, work through the ultimately exorcise a situation from his past that was causing him problems and creating mental and emotional blocks in the present. This he did, bravely and successfully, but asked me to pass on the warning to anyone who has suffered similarly in childhood, not to work with the malachite–quartz combination unless they are mentally and emotionally prepared for it!

Moonstone

I love the feel of moonstone on every level. It is an extremely tactile gem that just invites handling, and when worn or placed upon the skin seems to become part of it. I find it invaluable as a healing gem and as an emotional balancer. Used in combination with rose quartz I find it is excellent for all heart, lung and chest complaints.

Using these two gems and absent healing I had great success with a lady who was facing the possibility of a heart–lung transplant. She is now almost in full health, having completely baffled her consultants who, a little over a year ago, gave her no more than a few weeks to live unless she underwent major surgery.

Moonstone also works well with chronic bronchitis and emphysema, at the very least making the condition more stable and manageable and thereby improving the sufferer's quality of life on all levels.

It really comes into its own when dealing with feminine complaints, especially where the lady is a particularly emotional or nervous personality. I recommend it highly to all ladies who suffer any degree of discomfort at certain times of the month. I have had spectacular success using moonstone in combination with amazonite, jade and chrysocolla in treating severe and debilitating premenstrual tension and menopausal problems.

I always wear or carry moonstone before, during and for a day or so after menstruation and find that, apart from the general inconvenience, I have absolutely no emotional, physical or mental reaction to the natural hormonal fluctuations.

Obsidian Snowflake

Obsidian is another grounding and centring gem, with deeply mystical overtones. Holding it conjures up visions of the night, of immense star-scattered skies and ancient jungle temples and observatories. I can sense the stirring of the sleeping kundalini force in this gem, and its latent power.

I have used obsidian both as a grounding force and as a gateway during pathworking meditations, with remarkable and thought-provoking results.

Obsidian seems to bring me into alignment with myself on all levels; it is an anchor that allows plenty of scope for the boat above to drift freely where it will in complete safety.

It totally precludes negativity and calms a stressful situation or state of mind immediately.

I find that obsidian is a gem of intent and expression, in that if I am finding it difficult to express my inner thoughts and feelings, handing a piece of obsidian that I have been holding to the person I am trying to communicate with, enables them to pick up the gist of what I am saying and the deeper meaning behind my words.

On a physical level I use obsidian, like sodalite, in cases of shock, trauma or hysteria. I also find it good to settle an upset stomach, colic and nervous indigestion.

Rose Quartz

The mother of crystals! Warm, compassionate, forgiving and gentle, rose quartz is everything we would look for in an ideal mother. Everyone is drawn to the love that rose quartz radiates, for there is a child within us all, and I would not be without my rose quartz under any circumstances.

I have seen it work miracles on an emotional level; but often there is a certain amount of trauma to be worked through in the process.

An example of this is a client of mine who arrived one day with the suggestion from a colour therapist that she should obtain rose quartz purely for its beautiful pink hues. We had an immediate rapport, and I was struck by her quiet gentleness and composure.

A day or so later, I received a telephone call from her. She was in such great distress that she had been forced to leave her job and go home to the sanctuary of her bed.

Bit by bit, the whole story came tumbling out. All through her childhood she had suffered parental abuse necessitating years of therapy and counselling afterwards. She had thought herself finally free of all the hurt and bad memories, and believed she had learned not only to forgive her parents for what they had done, but also to forgive herself and release the self-blame she had harboured.

However, the rose quartz had gently brought to the surface these deepest hurts, that she and her counsellors had been unable to reach. Reliving them again was making her almost suicidal and certainly she was terrified. Throughout it all, she spoke of the presence of the rose quartz 'as big as a house' in her dreams and in her mind's eye. I calmed her as best I could and told her that this situation would not continue for longer than 48 hours, but that I was available at all times if she felt she needed me.

Several days passed without a word from her, and as I did not have a telephone number for her I was beginning to feel rather worried.

However, she eventually turned up on my doorstep looking fresh, radiant and 10 years younger. At last she was completely free and cleansed of her experiences thanks to the rose quartz.

She has since sent several pieces to her friends and to her counsellor with an account of her experience, and I understand that many others have been helped by this sympathetic therapist who, through the rose quartz, is now introducing crystals as part of her healing programme.

Rutilated Quartz

This crystal really buzzes! I find that it has a dynamic energy that is slightly more aggressive, in the nicest possible sense, than clear quartz.

I do not often use it in healing as it can be rather a handful for sensitive clients to cope with. Again, I find that it has a superb 'drawing out' quality, whether it be on a purely physical level or an encouraging people to open up to their feelings and expressing themselves with clarity and insight. Used over the third eye in meditation it can greatly accentuate spiritual vision and help intuitive interpretation.

I carry a piece if I am in a situation that necessitates self-projection and self-confidence, as I find that it helps me to access the inner calm and stored knowledge that tends to blank out on me under stress. It is excellent to boost energy levels and to clear the mind of clutter, enabling me to focus and concentrate upon the task at hand.

Smokey Quartz

I am very drawn to smokey quartz whatever the depth of shade that it may have. It has a solid, grounding, almost earthy feel; but I find it extremely powerful.

There seems to be more programme information in smokey quartz crystals than in clear quartz; I feel that it is of a highly secret, almost occult nature, with strong Atlantean connections.

I have quite often found tiny triangles etched into the facets of smokey quartz crystals. They seem to link up with the pyramids, not just in Egypt and the Americas, but also on Atlantis and, perhaps surprisingly, in mounds such as Silbury Hill in the United Kingdom.

Smokey quartz suggests the aspiration and wisdom

of men who built upwards to the heavens using the firm foundation of the earth. It tells us that while we are rooted in the physical, and are responsible for the perpetuity of life in human form, we can also build our spirituality as high as possible towards the Divine Seed from which we have all sprung.

Smokey quartz is deep and mysterious, but always sympathetic and accessible to the sincere seeker. On a physical level, I have used smokey quartz for its calming, almost sedative effect, for balancing sexual energy and polarity, for easing depression and stress headaches, and to calm an irritable bowel.

Sodalite

I find sodalite to be a no-nonsense, practical gem with considerable sedative qualities. Excellent to use in a first-aid context to allay panic attacks and surmount phobias, sodalite is essentially reassuring and powerfully protective.

I myself conquered a crippling fear of flying thanks to sodalite in combination with quartz and aquamarine.

It is cool, and takes the sting out of an explosive temperament, calms anger and eliminates fear.

I have heard it said that sodalite can be used in place of lapis lazuli in a healing context, but personally I do not agree. The two gems have completely differing 'feels' to them, and on any level of use, physical, mental or spiritual, their attributes are too unalike to be interchangeable.

Sodalite vibrates at a much lower, slower rate than lapis lazuli. When used in meditation it takes the subject only part of the way, and does not provide the insight into the meaning of the journey in the way that lapis does.

Again this is possibly indicative of my own shortcomings, but I have found that meditating with sodalite is a sure way of bringing on a deep and undisturbed sleep.

Tiger's Eye

In my limited experience most people either love or loathe tiger's eye! I cannot say that it really moves me one way or another, but I do find that it is not first to spring to mind either for healing or in any spiritual context.

I have done very little work with tiger's eye, so cannot really pass much comment upon it. It has an indifferent feel to it, and I am unable to make a strong connection to it on an intuitive level.

Tourmaline

An invaluable troubleshooter, tourmaline has a high level of resonance, a strong pulse and vibrance, that immediately pushes up awareness and energy on all levels.

I find that tourmaline is invaluable for clearing congestion and blockages in the etheric body, for strengthening and energising the chakras, and for bringing all levels of being into alignment.

In my work with tourmaline, I have found that there are no hard and fast rules as to how or where it should be used upon the body. It seems to be self-directive, going at once to the source of the problem which may, at first sight, be completely unrelated to the presenting symptoms.

I would use tourmaline to scan the aura, chakras and body of a patient if my pendulum was not to hand. You can feel a change in vibrationary pitch in tourmaline as it is passed over 'hot spots' and it works extremely harmoniously in partnership with quartz.

Turquoise

Although I am not personally drawn to turquoise, I have gained a healthy respect for it through the work we have done together. I find that it is excellent for headaches, perhaps the most powerful of gems to use in this context, no matter whether the pain is organic, stress related or as a result of injury.

Like malachite and aventurine, turquoise is wonderful for the eyes, and a lotion made by steeping any or a combination of all of these gems in distilled water makes a refreshing and soothing eye wash. Turquoise has a rather astringent feel to it. It is certainly toning and revitalising, and a few pieces wrapped in a muslin bag and held under the cold tap while drawing a bath really adds zest and freshness to the water.

I have found that turquoise readily lends itself to gemstone combinations, and always feels fresh, eager and willing to help and heal. Perhaps the most enthusiastic gemstone!

CHAPTER 6

Pyramids

For thousands of years, pyramids have fascinated scholars, archaeologists and lay-people alike. An aura of mystery has always surrounded them.

The ancient Egyptians were not the only people to build pyramids. In South and Central America, for example, a number of large pyramids have been discovered.

It is thought that some of the Atlantean priests who escaped from Atlantis when it was destroyed eventually found themselves in South America and re-recreated the pyramidical technology which they had known when living in Atlantis. It is also believed that there were several very large crystal pyramids in the ancient continent of Atlantis. These pyramids were used by the priesthood as temples for sacred rituals.

Outwardly, the walls of these crystal pyramids appeared solid but if the priest wished to gain entry inside the pyramid he would have to place his hand upon a certain part of the wall and a doorway would open up in front of him. The pyramid doorway would be protected by unique vibrational energies and if the priest's vibrations were not recognised by the doorway then he would not be able to gain admittance.

When Atlantis was destroyed, those priests who were allowed to leave were spirited to the four corners of the world taking their knowledge with them to their new civilisations.

*   *   *   *

Most of the pyramids are, of course, to be found in Egypt. According to historians and archaeologists, the Pyramid Age of Egypt began with the Third Dynasty (2686 BC). During this Pyramid Age around 80 pyramids were constructed. Many of them are no longer immediately recognisable as pyramids as they have been reduced to little more than sand and rubble, but the Egyptian archaeologists, through years of painstaking research and work, have managed to identify where most of these pyramids would once have stood.

Throughout the years, however, considerable controversy has arisen over the question of precisely why the pyramids were built in the first place.

Egyptologists claim that the pyramids were erected simply as tombs; while other archaeologists, excavating pyramids in South America, have advanced the theory that they were really used as temples. Recently, some pyramidologists have stated that they believe the pyramids are possibly resonators, or storehouses, of energy. Certainly, this is an explanation that is attracting increasing support.

The theory put forward by these pyramidologists is that the frequencies radiated by the earth itself (including the magnetic force lines) together with cosmic radiation, blend within the pyramidical structure and produce a beat frequency (in the same way in which two piano keys, when struck simultaneously, produce a third, or beat, frequency). It is thought by some pyramidologists that this beat frequency could create an energy radiation.

My own view, from research that I have undertaken with past-life regression, has tended to confirm that the main purpose of the pyramids, apart from housing the bodies of the Pharaohs, was to be used as temples by the priesthood. I also believe that, in some way, the pyramids were used to transmit and store cosmic energy.

Max Toth and Greg Nielsen, in their book *Pyramid Power*, says:

'There is no doubt that every civilisation which built pyramids did so with the use of highly advanced mathematical and astronomical calculations and a seemingly impossible mastery of the skill of stone masonry. In civilisations separated not only by thousands of miles but also by hundreds of years, stones weighing many tons were hoisted into position with infinite precision for the purpose of erecting pyramidical structures.'

*   *   *   *

Because of the equally advanced levels of both skill and science used in the erection of the Egyptian pyramids, it would seem highly possible that the pyramid builders were taught by people from other civilisations.

If so, where did these outsiders come from? How did they get there? Did they teach astronomy and mathematics for the sole purpose of having the pyramids constructed? Or was there some other motive behind the endowment of this knowledge upon the people of these ancient civilisations?

And despite our present-day knowledge of building technology and techniques the world's most advanced building construction company would have tremendous difficulty in constructing a pyramid today that would equal, let alone surpass, the pyramids that were erected so long ago.

The largest pyramid of all, and one that is still standing, is the Great Pyramid of Giza.

The Great Pyramid is also known as the Pyramid of Cheops, Cheops being a Pharaoh who reigned in the Fourth Dynasty (around 2450 BC). The pyramid is 481 feet high and 756 feet square at its base and is a mathematical phenomenon.

The Great Pyramid was the seventh wonder of the ancient world. It consists of some 2,500,000 limestone blocks, each weighing between two and 70 tons. These blocks, which require two tons of pressure on a diamond bit merely to drill a hole into it, are cut with a tolerance of one-thousandth of an inch, and fit together like a jigsaw puzzle.

The pyramid is built on the exact mathematical ratio of Pi 3.14159, the ratio of a circle's circumference to its diameter. It has been calculated by mathematicians that if, during its construction, ten of these stones were piled with precision on top of each other every day, some 500 tons a day on average, the pyramid would have taken about 250,000 days, or 664 years, to build. We should also bear in mind that, officially anyway, the true value of Pi was not discovered until 600 years ago!

The Great Pyramid's four triangular faces incline at an angle of approximately 51 degrees, 51 minutes and 51 seconds to the ground. The entire Great Pyramid was originally oriented in line with true north.

Max Toth and Greg Nielsen also say in their book:

'So great was the engineering agility and skill required to manoeuvre the huge granite blocks into place that how it was accomplished still remains a mystery.

Even more mysterious, however, is where these blocks were stored prior to the burial of the Pharaoh; or, if the blocks were placed before the internment took place, how the body was entombed with the plugs blocking the entrance way to the burial chamber. Many theories have been offered to explain these mysteries, all too implausible to be given consideration. To this day, the granite plugs remain in place, a mute testimony to the genius of the Pharaoh's architect.'

*   *   *   *

The Greek historian, Herodotus, who visited Egypt in the fifth century BC, nearly 2,000 years after the Great Pyramid was alleged to have been built, wrote that it was constructed over a timespan of 20 years by 400,000 labourers who would have been divided into four groups of 100,000 men, and each group would only have worked on its construction for a period of three months in any one year.

However, Herodotus was not able to explain the logistical problems of how the Egyptian officials provided food, shelter, and sanitation facilities for all these 100,000 labourers, nor was there any evidence that they did so!

Arguments and controversy have always surrounded

the Great Pyramid of Giza, and probably always will. For although most Egyptologists, scientists and scholars do agree that the Great Pyramid was built by the Pharaoh Cheops, somewhere between 2686 and 2181, many favouring the year 2450 BC, there is no definite evidence that the pyramid was actually built then; and most psychics, sensitives and seers, believe that it was built many thousands of years before 2450 BC and was used for purposes other than as a tomb.

*   *   *   *

Edgar Cayce who, between the years 1920 and 1944 gave many thousands of 'life-readings', said in one of his readings that the Great Pyramid was actually built more than 10,000 years ago by priests and priestesses from Atlantis. Edgar Cayce himself believed that he was a priest in Atlantis named 'Ra-Ta' and that when Atlantis was destroyed he was spirited to Egypt in order to help found a new civilisation – the pre-Dynasty era of Egyptian history.

My own experiences in regressing people back to ancient civilisations have led me to believe that there were a number of crystal pyramids built in Atlantis and that the technology for the creation of the Great Pyramid at Giza, and all subsequent Egyptian and South American pyramids, was introduced into our world by priests and priestesses from Atlantis who were able to escape at the time of the final destruction. If we accept this theory then obviously the Great Pyramid at Giza was constructed many thousands of years prior to the reign of Pharaoh Cheops!

Edgar Cayce says that the Great Pyramid at Giza was not constructed solely as a means of housing the tomb of Cheops but as a place where records could be stored; a virtual history of mankind. It is said that many of these records were written down in a mixture of hieroglyphics and Atlantean script.

An old legend suggests that there are still some subterranean chambers to be discovered under the Great Pyramid and that these chambers contain valuable artefacts and writings relating to a period of our history, long gone. When they are discovered, as I believe they will be, they will provide incontrovertible proof that the Great Pyramid was created thousands of years before the reign of Cheops.

Other pyramids too, like the one said to contain the mummified body of the Pharaoh Akhnaton, are also supposed to contain esoteric writings and records. It is written that when the right people are present, and the time is right, those records will be discovered.

*   *   *   *

Manly P. Hall in *The Secret Teachings of All Ages* alleges that the pyramid was constructed by people arriving from Atlantis after it had been destroyed. He proposes the theory that the Atlanteans established centres of education and learning, built in the form of pyramidical temples, in which they hid their esoteric secrets which were written in symbolic language, to be discovered and understood only by those who were worthy of acquiring and using this sacred knowledge.

According to Hall, there is a great mystical knowledge hidden within the inner depths of the pyramid. The square base means that the pyramid is solidly founded on nature, and its immutable laws; the angles represent silence,

Figure 1. Pyramid Meditation.

profundity, intelligence and truth. The south side of the pyramid signifies cold, the north side represents heat, the west side symbolises darkness and the east side, light. The triangular sides typify the three-fold spiritual power. Hall goes on to say that he is certain that there is a secret room or chamber within the pyramid that will one day be rediscovered.

Many people have talked and speculated about Atlantis and its effect upon the future of mankind. Many writers and seers, including Edgar Cayce, have told of the vast corruption in Atlantis – the endless quest for untold power sought by certain priests – that eventually led to its final destruction.

*   *   *   *

It is important to realise that Atlantis is far more than some fiction writer's fantasy. It is not just an idealistic figment of someone's imagination. Atlantis really did exist. Plato, in his book *Critias* described Atlantis, which apparently was once known as Poseidonis. In his book, Plato observed that the high point of the Atlantean civilisation occurred when Gods walked with men.

Many mystical and esoteric teachings continually refer to the idea that Atlantean knowledge and records are hidden within secret chambers still to be discovered in the pyramids and that one day these chambers will be opened by people who are deemed worthy of being entrusted with all this sacred and spiritual knowledge.

It could happen that when the time is right the same people who had access to this sacred and spiritual knowledge and who have now reincarnated in new bodies in this incarnation will once again return to the pyramids and enter these secret chambers.

As we know that the prime cause of the destruction of Atlantis was man's total disregard for the ethical and moral standards of natural law, we can understand how important it is that any information and data that is discovered, and which can be understood, is not allowed to fall into the wrong hands. Otherwise history may repeat itself!

*   *   *   *

It is worth recounting the strange experience of Dr Paul Brunton described in his book, *A Search in Secret Egypt*. After lengthy negotiations with the Egyptian bureaucratic hierarchy, Dr Brunton succeeded in obtaining permission to spend a night alone inside the King's Chamber of the Great Pyramid.

Dr Brunton says that on entering the King's Chamber he found a marble slab next to the large coffer which, incidentally, is exactly aligned on the north–south axis.

He had had some training in the Egyptian religion and was also quite knowledgeable about some of the more recent discoveries in parapsychology. He had, therefore, prepared himself by fasting for three days before his night in the pyramid. This put him in a receptive frame of mind to experience whatever phenomenon existed there.

Sitting with his back to the great coffer, Dr Brunton decided to turn off his flashlight. Although he could sense a negative presence and was experiencing a strong urge to leave the chamber, he forced himself to stand firm, even though grotesque and deformed entities flitted in and out of the chamber, goading his sensibility and sanity. It took every ounce of courage that he possessed to fight off his fear. The combination of darkness and the negative presences convinced him that he would never spend another night alone in the Great Pyramid.

Then, as suddenly as the negative atmosphere had come, it vanished. He felt, at first, a friendly air come alive in the chamber. Next, he could see in front of him two figures, who both looked like high priests and suddenly, inside his head, he heard one of the priests asking him why he had come and if the world of mortals was not enough for him. Brunton answered, 'No, that cannot be.' The priest replied, 'The way of dream will draw thee far far from the fold of reason. Some have gone upon it and come back mad.

Turn now, whilst there is yet time and follow the path appointed for mortal feet.'

Brunton insisted that he must stay. The priest who had spoken to him then turned and disappeared. The other priest asked Brunton to lie upon the coffer. Suddenly a force came over him and within a few seconds he was hovering outside his body. He was in another dimension of less stress and strain. He could see a silver cord connecting his new body with the one lying on the coffer. He became aware of a feeling of freedom.

Later, Brunton found himself with the second priest who told him that he must return with a message: 'Know, my son, that in this ancient temple lies the lost record of the early races of man and of the covenant which they made with the Creator through the first of His great prophets. Know, too, that chosen men were brought here of old to be shown this covenant that they might return to their fellows and keep the secret alive. Take back with thee the warning that when men foresake their Creator and look on their fellows with hate, as with the princes of Atlantis, in whose time this pyramid was built, they are destroyed by the weight of their own iniquity, even as the people of Atlantis were destroyed.'

As the priest finished speaking, Brunton suddenly found himself back in his own body. He felt it to be cumbersome compared to the one he had just inhabited. He got up, put on his jacket and checked his watch. It was exactly midnight, the hour that is customarily associated with strange events.

*   *   *   *

Patrick Flanagan, well-known in America for his scientific and inventive genius, claims to have found the ancient secret of prolonging life.

'Death comes about as a result of decay,' he says 'History is full of phenomena which may have been caused by biocosmic energy. Examples are the Egyptian mummies, the biblical Ark of the Covenant and the story of Methuselah, who lived for 969 years.

Biocosmic energy is the very essence of life force itself, this energy has been known to exist but, until now, no one has been able to isolate it. The Great Pyramid of Giza, the seventh wonder of the world, is at last revealed to the world for its true purpose, a very powerful source of biocosmic energy.

The word pyramid itself reveals its most hidden secret. Pyramid means quite literally, "fire in the middle".'

Patrick Flanagan goes on to say that this 'fire in the middle' is the long sought-after biocosmic energy. Flanagan has also discovered that not only has the pyramid an accumulation of energy inside but it also radiates energy off the points and top. The pyramid actually works better when the top is slightly flattened, as is the case with the Great Pyramid of Giza.

It has always been believed that the flat tops of the pyramids once contained a 24-carat gold quartz capstone. This would also have added considerably to the pyramid's storehouse of power and energy. Sadly, in the passage of time, all these powerful cap-stones have been vandalised and removed.

*   *   *   *

A few years ago, a Frenchman by the name of Monsieur Bovis, paid a visit to the Great Pyramid of Giza. There were some rubbish containers in the King's Chamber in which Bovis could see various dead cats and other small animals which had apparently wandered into the Pyramid and died of starvation.

There was something very strange about these corpses: there was no smell of decay at all! His curiosity aroused, Bovis examined the animals very carefully and discovered that they were dehydrated and mummified, despite the humidity in the King's Chamber.

Bovis pondered this apparent conundrum and wondered whether the pyramidical shape itself could have been responsible for this natural embalming process. So he made a wooden scale model of the Great Pyramid of Cheops with a base three feet long, and oriented it to true north like the Great Pyramid.

Inside his model, one third of the way up, he placed the body of a dead cat which had only recently died. After a few days, it became mummified. Bovis then experimented by placing other organic materials in the model, particularly matter that usually decays very quickly, such as calf's brains, and when these failed to putrefy, he concluded that there must be something about the shape of the pyramid which prevents decay and causes dehydration.

*   *   *   *

A Czechoslovakian radio engineer called Karel Drbal obtained, by chance, a copy of Bovis's reports and decided to make some further experiments with models of pyramids. His conclusions were, 'there is a definite relationship between the shape of the space inside the pyramid, and the physical, chemical and biological processes going on inside that space'.

Drbal also considered that the pyramidical shape might also be responsible for an accumulation of electro-magnetic waves or cosmic rays, or of some unknown energy. Placing a used razor blade within a six inch high model of Cheops' Pyramid, oriented true north, Drbal found that the edges of the blade automatically recovered their sharpness after use and that he could shave with one razor blade as many as 200 times!

He believed that the environment inside the pyramid somehow made the crystals in the blade return to their original form. Drbal was issued with Czech patent number 91304, after a long fight, for the Cheops' Pyramid Razor Blade Sharpener.

An Italian milk company has started putting their milk into pyramid shaped cartons. They have discovered that milk keeps indefinitely without refrigeration. A French company have even patented a pyramidical container for selling yoghurt.

In March 1963, biologists of the University of Oklahoma confirmed that the skin cells of the Egyptian Princess Mene were actually capable of living. Princess Mene has been dead for several thousand years!

*   *   *   *

In my healing room I used to have an eight foot high pyramid, in which I held all my crystal healing sessions. The results were extremely encouraging.

One young boy, eight and a half years old, was

brought to me by his distraught mother. He had been brain damaged from birth and could only walk with difficulty. All his motor movements were almost out of control and he was unable to talk at all.

I laid him down on my couch, directly under the apex of my pyramid. I placed some of my largest quartz crystals underneath the couch and took my laser wand in my right hand. For 30 minutes I directed healing energy from my laser wand into the young boy – he was bathed in beautiful crystalline light and energy.

The next day his mother telephoned me excitedly with the news that he was very different – and much more responsive – following his treatment. After a further three treatments he was almost walking normally, was making great efforts to talk and seemed much happier within himself. He may never be able to lead a totally normal life, but his improvement has been quite remarkable.

As a 'sensitive' myself I have always been very much aware of the difference in the energy field immediately I stepped inside my pyramid. It always has an immediate effect upon my nervous system and leads to a slowing down of my body metabolism rate. The pyramid appears to have the ability to amplify the unique energies present within the structure which create a wonderful healing power and energy.

*   *   *   *

Pyramids are also very effective for all forms of meditation. Many people claim that they experience feelings ranging from calmness to extreme euphoria during their meditation sessions inside their pyramid.

I always feel as if I am being lifted out of my body and levitated through space and time. So beautiful are these experiences that I am always extremely reluctant to come back into my physical body!

Most people who have experimented with large pyramids report that they start by experiencing a total relaxation of the body, followed by the shutting out of unnecessary external stimuli and irrelevant thoughts and finally achieving an altered state of consciousness which allows the individual to concentrate on deeper inner levels.

So many positive results can be obtained through using pyramids. We have so far only scratched the surface of what can be done. Pyramids may help you to reduce the level of stress and tension in your body. You may attain a heightened charge of psychic energy, increased memory recall, views of past incarnations, visions, dreams, indescribably beautiful colours, forms, shapes, symbols, or music 'from the spheres'. There are people who experience precognition, inter-planetary travel, telepathic communications, answers to prayers and overall revitalisation of their entire being.

From my own experience I have discovered that through working with my quartz crystals within the pyramidical structure I am able to substantially increase my own level of healing energy and vibrations – with excellent results.

My own eight-foot pyramid is constructed out of thickish copper tubing, copper being an excellent conductor of energy. I place four large quartz crystal clusters at the four corners of the pyramid which helps to balance the enormous energy field created. Most of my crystal healing treatments take place on my massage couch. The pyramid was designed so that the height of my massage couch (28 inches) is approximately one third the height of the pyramid's apex. The massage couch is also aligned on a true north/south axis.

Although I am only in the early days of experimentation and research into the different facets of pyramid energy and power, I am already discovering that this unique energy can be very powerful indeed.

CHAPTER 7

Akhnaton – The 'Heretic' Pharaoh

Akhnaton, known as the heretic pharaoh of the 18th dynasty, was believed to have been the reincarnation of the last Atlantean high priest. He possessed great knowledge, wisdom and understanding together with an immense power of devotion which he directed to the one God, whose sheer beauty and majesty overwhelmed him and whom Akhnaton saw as the power behind the sun.

Mona Rolfe, the Irish seer, in her book *Initiation By The Nile* gives us a wonderful insight into Akhnaton's character and personality:

She says, 'To Akhnaton the sun was the most glorious sight and he wanted all men to share in his knowledge. He believed that if he could build the perfect city and a temple that would be supreme in its glory, then men would see it as an expression of truth and recognise the value and worth of the teaching.

Akhnaton was a genius, a great soul who drew his inspiration direct from God. To him the sun was the most glorious sight of all. But he did not worship the sun, he worshipped the one invisible God – whose symbol the sun was.

He was hated by the priesthood when he sought to effect changes in the form of worship in the Temples. He realised the necessity for the multiplicity of Gods, that each one had his place. But he knew that there was one God above them all – and that he could communicate direct with God in the silence of his own heart. He told the priests that all men could communicate direct with God – and this they did not like; they did not wish to have the power taken out of their own hands, for they had accumulated great wealth through the power that they held.

Many souls who are incarnate today are incarnate from bodies which they held in the time of Akhnaton. Through study, meditation and concentration, at this moment the incidents in which we were concerned can be built through our ancient memory, and in remembering we may not only help to bring to light knowledge which will be of importance to the archaeologists and others, but also will link the path of our own soul with the paths of others who trod the self same way with us during that particular dynasty. You believe that the tomb of Akhnaton has been discovered and all that was in it has been revealed. This is not so!

His tomb lies as yet untouched, undisturbed, three storeys down below ground level of the Temple of Thebes. Many discoveries will be made of the first layer of that ancient temple, much will be found of the second layer dealing with matters concerning the Great Atlantean Temple; then, at the third layer, shall we find this vast and glorious temple within which the body of Akhnaton is held in reverence and light.

Although the tomb is very deep below the level of the sea, there is no sign of damp, of mildew, or the ravages of creatures.

The tomb itself is made of transparent stone, stone which was used in the great temple of Atlantis and in Persia for the healing beds; in some lights it looks of one colour only; in others it looks of many colours; the rays of the Place of Light pass through it and enfold it, beating their power into the earth, drawing from the sand a great light and using it for the preparation of yet further rays, which will eventually guide those who hold the key to the tomb.

None other may approach it!

The coffins, or sarcophagi, lie side by side one another; in the one the magnificent figure of Akhnaton and in the other lies the figure of Hareth, his wife; and that you may know she is Hareth when you hear of her finding, you will remember that about the brow she bears a golden circlet, wide, soft, which though restraining the tresses it leaves no impress upon the delicate brow itself. In the centre of that golden band is a mighty ruby, shining as no ruby you have ever seen before. The hands are delicate, cared for and beautiful.

The bodies of Hareth and Akhnaton look as they looked in life – no decomposition, no fading of the tissue, no darkening of the colour of the skin, for the preservation of these bodies is perfect; only when the light of day strikes them do they crumble into dust. But they will not crumble until their proof is established and all those who have the right to do so have been permitted to look upon the features of one of the greatest and most important Kings of earth, whose soul left the Place of Light and through many incarnations reached the body of a Prince, to serve as a King and to pass back to the Place of Light again.

For to understand our past lives we must pray to Akhnaton; he has the clue. Sometimes that information will be passed through to you by our doorkeeper, or by someone who is permitted for you to read the Akashic record of the past; but only to those who hold the Silver Ankh in a certain position as proof that they have the right to read it, only to these will be given the privilege and the power.

Outside the tomb, at either end, will be discovered two small chambers, so small that a man would have difficulty in standing upright therein – but these are merely boxes of records.

In the box placed at the head of the young King and Hareth will be found a manuscript in ancient script giving the clue to the last book of Genesis; in the other will be found a script in Aramaic, but written along before anyone speaking Aramaic approached the Court of Egypt.

These scripts will need special readers. Only one or two, who have been trained under the guidance of Oneferu, will be able to read them. Only these will be able to place them in their proper position in the Book of Genesis and in that last book which should follow the writing of the Revelation of St John – the book which closes that book of Scriptures which you know as your Bible.

The pathway to the tomb is in darkness; man must traverse the temple and many passages before he reaches the tomb; and the passages are sown with white stones – the white stone representing the Light of the Spirit, stones just large enough for a man to hold in the palm of his hand.

When the right man treads the passage the stones

lift, the light shines and he walks forward to the tomb itself, where he will be called upon to worship. For God in His Holiness is the guide and strength of mankind, the director of the life of man and the mighty works of God.'

*   *   *   *

Several other esoteric sources refer to the fact that records providing detailed information on Atlantean technology will one day be discovered in a secret chamber within the tomb of Akhnaton.

Also often referred to is the idea that Akhnaton's tomb – and the hidden secret chambers – will only be discovered when the right person or persons are present.

H. C. Randall-Stevens (El Eros) in his book, *Atlantis to the Latter Days*, says:

'Akhnaton maintained one shrine to Aton, at Thebes, and this shrine was built almost entirely underground, and was walled in all around. None were allowed near and its secrets were never known after his death. It was entered by a series of secret doors moved by levers, and it was to this place that his followers conveyed his dead body, so that it should escape desecration at the hands of the priests of Amen.

These subterranean chambers shall again be uncovered, and it will be seemingly by accident that one of the secret levers will be moved.

The body of Akhnaton will be found two chambers down in a room which appears round, but which is, in reality, octagonal. This chamber is inscribed with prayers and songs to Atanu-Ra, the one God of Light and Life.

The body lies in an alabaster and gold sarcophagus,

and near it will be found the ossified remains of a young woman. These are the remains of the chief singer Hareesh, who, having secretly borne the King a son, who afterwards ruled the double empire as Tut-ankh-Amen, threw herself into the Nile waters, thinking to find rest with Atanu-Ra, where she intended to wait the coming of her lover, Akhnaton.'

*　　*　　*　　*

If these ancient writings are to be believed then we are rapidly approaching the time when all will be revealed. At present Akhnaton is one of only two pharaohs whose mummified body has yet to be found.

My own view is that when his tomb is eventually uncovered the circumstances surrounding its discovery will have an even greater impact upon the world than when Howard Carter stumbled across the tomb of Tutankhamen in 1923.

CHAPTER 8

The Chakras

The word 'chakra' is derived from the sanskrit word meaning wheel. If we were able to see chakras (as many seers and psychics do) we would see a wheel of energy continuously revolving or rotating each chakra at a different speed.

One of the reasons that people fall ill is because their chakras become out of alignment, they are 'imbalanced' or there are blockages which restrict the free flow of the body's energy.

There are seven major chakras. For simplicity I intend to concentrate upon these seven. They are as follows:

First Chakra   – base of the spine
Second Chakra – spleen, or sexual centre
Third Chakra   – solar plexus
Fourth Chakra – heart
Fifth Chakra   – throat
Sixth Chakra   – third eye
Seventh Chakra – crown

These chakras all play an active role in all our crystal healing treatments.

Any imbalances within any chakra may have profound effects upon either our physical or physiological bodies. We can use our quartz crystals to rebalance our chakric centres and once they have been properly balanced then the body will gradually return to normal.

First Chakra

The first chakra is located at the bottom of the spine. This is where the kundalini is situated. This chakra is associated with the colour red. It is a very important centre as it has so much effect upon the rest of the body. I find that I can release a great deal of the physical stress and tension of the nervous system by working on the base chakra with my quartz crystals.

Second Chakra

The second chakra is located within an area bounded by the spleen and sexual centre. This chakra is associated with the colour orange. Usually people suffering from sexual blockages need healing here.

Third Chakra

The third chakra is the solar plexus and is located just below the navel. This chakra is associated with the colour yellow. There is often a great amount of physical energy and power within this chakra or emanating from it. This chakra is also the psychic storehouse of mystical energy and is the energy centre used by materialisation mediums for producing ectoplasm and other psychic manifestations.

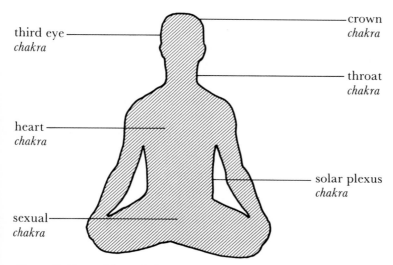

Figure 2. View of front chakras.

Fourth Chakra

The fourth chakra is the heart centre. It is located in an area in the centre of the chest, between the two nipples. The colours associated with this chakra are green and pink. I use the heart chakra to help people suffering from emotional trauma and problems in their relationships. I find that by using a piece of rose quartz I am able to help release their inner emotional tension and trauma.

Fifth Chakra

The fifth chakra is the throat centre. It is located in an area which corresponds to the centre of the throat. The colours associated with this chakra are either blue or turquoise. When people suffer from headaches (perhaps migraine) and tension within the neck and shoulder muscles I find that often the basic cause is that the throat chakra has become blocked.

Sixth Chakra

The sixth chakra is the third eye. This chakra is located on the forehead between the eyebrows. The colour most associated with this chakra is purple. When helping people to develop their own spiritual intuition I find that amethyst, sodalite, lapis lazuli or sugilite are ideal stones with which to work.

Seventh Chakra

The seventh chakra is the crown centre. This chakra is located on the top of the head. The colour associated with this chakra is white. During any crystal healing session this chakra needs to be open. It is the chakra through which you obtain the highest understanding and knowledge.

To balance the chakras I use the following technique. With the patient lying on his back I place two quartz crystals on the third eye chakra, points facing downwards. I then place two quartz crystals on the palm, points upwards; two quartz crystals on the breast area, points upwards; and two quartz crystals placed on the top of the thighs, point upwards.

If the patient lies quietly on his back for about 15 minutes, the chakras will quickly re-align themselves.

CHAPTER 9

Crystal Wands

Crystal wands are one of the most powerful 'light tools' currently known to mankind. The wand itself consists of a hollow copper tube of about 12 inches in length. The copper tube should be around ¾" in diameter.

A quartz crystal at least three inches long and around ¾" wide, clear and with reasonably unchipped facets, should be affixed to one end of the copper tube. At the other end of the tube is affixed either a copper cap or another quartz crystal.

Either single- or double-terminated quartz crystals may be used. The whole copper tube is insulated by a leather strip wound completely around the wand.

The best way to discover exactly how a crystal wand functions – and its tremendous potential as an energiser – is to make one for yourself. By constructing your own crystal wand you will find that it becomes much easier to merge your own vibrations with that of your wand.

To make your own crystal wand first take your hollow copper tube and, with a hacksaw, cut two lengthwise strips at one end of the tube, about three inches deep. Then, with a pair of pliers, bend the sides outwards to allow room for your quartz crystal to slide into place.

Glue the sides of your quartz crystal and then gently slide it into its place within the copper tube. Bend the sides back into place ensuring that at least one inch of your crystal protrudes at the end. At the other end of the copper tube, either glue the copper cap into position or affix another quartz crystal.

Finally, take your leather strip, which should be about three feet in length, and place a small amount of glue at intervals along one side. Then tightly wrap the leather, in spiral fashion, around the copper tubing. Your crystal wand is now ready.

When your crystal wand is lying by itself it is in passive mode but as soon as you pick it up it becomes operational or in active mode. Crystal wands are extremely simple to operate. All you need to do is to pick up your wand, focus the crystalline energy by visualising a blue-white light of energy radiating from the apex of the quartz crystal in your wand, and you have created your own powerful ray of energy and power. You must be sure to use your new tool wisely.

At my first crystal healing workshop, when I had only just constructed my first crystal wand, I was holding it in my hand while I was talking and, without thinking, I must have directed the wand at the third eye chakra of one of the students present. With a yell the student nearly toppled back on his chair. Apparently he had experienced a tremendous burst of energy and power emanating from my wand which had almost thrown him back into his seat!

Be very careful, therefore, where you point your crystal wand when you are holding it.

Figure 3. Crystal Wand.

For ordinary crystal healing purposes I use my wand in much the same way as a normal quartz crystal. Holding it in my right hand I move the wand around the perimeter of the patient's body, in a clockwise direction, for a few moments. I then focus the energies of the wand through the apex of the quartz crystal and directly into the body of the person I am treating. I find that about 15 minutes is sufficient at any one time.

After directing the healing energy into the patient I finish by moving the wand around the perimeter of the patient's body, again in a clockwise direction, for a few moments. Using this technique the patient's body becomes surrounded by a field of crystalline energy which penetrates every fibre of the patient's inner and outer being and, in most cases, deep, lasting healing occurs.

As soon as I pick up my crystal wand it begins to vibrate and pulsate. My hands start to tingle and I feel alive with crystalline energy and power. I channel my own healing energies into the wand which then amplifies them further and by the time the healing rays leave the crystal at the end of the wand I can sense that I have created a wonderful source of power and energy.

I am often asked at my workshops and seminars why it is necessary to insulate the wand with leather. Insulation is essential for the user's own protection as I have found out from painful experience. When you are working with a crystal wand for any length of time a great many subatomic particles accumulate within the copper tube and, sometimes, if you touch the actual copper you may receive an electrical-type shock. This has happened to me on more than one occasion.

The results you obtain by using a crystal wand depend upon your own ability to attune yourself at a high enough level with all the vibrational energies at your disposal. Like everything else in life, the more you practise, the more you achieve. As your energies become stronger, your wand will grow more potent. Crystal wands never breakdown, never need an external power source and can be used 24 hours a day, seven days a week. The possibilities are unlimited. Experiment with your crystal wand. Stretch your imagination and inventiveness beyond their normal range. Allow yourself to become at one with your crystal wand. Establish a complete rapport and empathy with it.

Crystal wands may be used for purposes other than healing. For example, one evening I had to give a talk at a town some 50 miles from where I live. I was running late; I had been delayed and I knew that time was short. I came off the motorway and found myself engulfed in traffic held up by a continuous stream of red traffic lights.

My crystal wand happened to be lying on the passenger seat next to me. Without really thinking about what I was doing I idly picked up the wand and focused it on the next red traffic light that I came to. It turned to green immediately as did the next set of lights and the one after that! It continued in the same way, every red traffic light turning to green as soon as I directed the crystal wand at it and I managed to arrive at my meeting dead on time. Strange, but true!

Why not construct your own crystal wand and discover for yourself all that it can do?

CHAPTER 10

Crystal Massage

Crystal massage can be a beautiful and uplifting experience. It works on a deep esoteric level and not only does the physical body enjoy total relaxation but all the inner emotional stresses are brought skilfully to the surface of the mind – and dissipated.

For many years I have practised as both a qualified massage therapist and as a qualified tutor of massage. My massage treatments have involved several different kinds of massage ranging from Swedish massage to intuitive massage. When I began using crystals in my healing work it seemed perfectly natural that I should also use crystals as an extension of my massage treatments.

There are many and various ways of using crystals to enrich and enhance the massage experience. Besides massage I also practice aromatherapy (the ancient art of using and blending essential oils in massage treatments). I often use quartz crystals to increase the potency of the essential oils.

Having chosen and blended the most suitable combination of oils for my patient, I take my control quartz crystal and move it in a clockwise direction around the bottle containing the oil. This strengthens the bio-magnetic field around the bottle. I then take the lid off the bottle and direct the crystalline energies directly on to the oil. The oil is then ready for use.

In my own experience I have found that I am able to give a much more therapeutic treatment – and the patient responds a great deal more readily – as a result of using crystals in my aromatherapy sessions.

However, the pure delight in using a single-terminated quartz crystal with unchipped or polished facets, directly upon the patient's body, should never be underestimated!

Using a single-terminated crystal, crystal massage may be divided into two main categories:

1) Where a basic knowledge of massage techniques is essential.

2) Where it is unnecessary to have any knowledge of massage at all.

In the first category I prepare the patient in exactly the same way as if they were going to have an ordinary massage. I use my massage couch and the patient begins the session by lying on the stomach so that I can start by working on the back area. I always use massage oils on the patient first and their massage session proceeds in the usual way. When I have completed the basic massage treatment I pick up my quartz crystal and, very gently, massage the patient's entire body by stroking the single-terminated end of the quartz crystal across the skin. I start with the feet, move

Crystal Massage

slowly upwards to the head and then back down the entire body again.

The secret of giving a successful crystal massage lies in being able to control the quartz crystal so that it almost glides over the surface of the patient's skin. However, before you begin to use your quartz crystal it is important that you first programme it with the thought that the crystal vibrations and energies are going to merge with that of your patient.

I always mentally attune myself with the crystal by asking that the crystal energies be absorbed into the skin of the patient and that the body be totally re-energised, re-harmonised and re-balanced.

In the second category of crystal massage it is not necessary to have any basic knowledge at all. Instead of

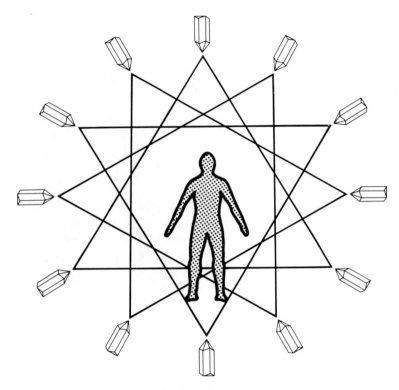

Figure 4. Crystal Massage Configuration.

using oils and hand massage techniques you move straight
on to using the quartz crystal. The effects can often be
absolutely delightful for your patient. As you progress and
become more experienced in crystal massage you will
become able to massage the patient's body, mind and spirit
at the same time, and once you have mastered ordinary
crystal massage techniques you can move on to practising
more advanced techniques.

For these more advanced techniques I dispense with my
massage couch altogether and use the floor. By working

with the patient on the floor not only do you have more room in which to work but the floor gives greater opportunities for using new forms of crystal configurations.

The patient lies on his or her back in the middle of the floor. I then place between 12 and 30 large quartz crystals, with all the single-terminated points facing inwards, around the patient's body. I try to place all the crystals equidistant points around the patient's body in a circular fashion allowing me enough room in which I can massage the patient and also remain inside the circle myself. The energy field thus created is exceptionally strong and the energies from each crystal combine to provide a unified magnetic energy field which penetrates every fibre of the patient's being.

Working on a patient who is lying within this energy field is a joyful experience as both patient and therapist are able to share in the wonderful relaxing vibrations that continue to emanate from the crystals while the treatment is progressing. A deep therapeutic crystal massage will often lead to the inner release of emotional traumas and tensions; of which the patient may have been completely unaware.

Many therapists have never used crystals in their massage treatments. In the future I hope that there will be a gradual awakening of interest and that more and more people will discover the exciting and beautiful world of crystal massage.

CHAPTER 11

Crystal Configurations

There are many crystal configurations and I am indebted to my friend and colleague, Frank Alper of the Arizona Metaphysical Society, for introducing me to this powerful and potent form of crystal healing.

In his trilogy of books, Exploring Atlantis, he describes many important healing methods – including the crystal configurations – which were once practised by the priests of Atlantis. Since first meeting Frank several years ago I have been using various crystal configurations in nearly all my healing treatments, as well as demonstrating them at my workshops, seminars and courses.

Randall and Vicki Baer, in their book entitled *The Crystal Connection*, include many, very powerful, advanced crystal configurations and gridworks. In most instances they are all extremely complex and beyond the understanding of most people. I hope to maintain simplicity in all that I am about to share with you.

One of the most effective crystal configurations, and one which I use frequently, is the 12-crystal configuration.

For this configuration you need 12 quartz crystals: two larger ones weighing between one pound and two pounds each and 10 smaller crystals, each at least three inches long and about one and a half inches wide.

While it is possible to use a massage couch I much prefer to use the floor as there is more room to spread out.

Instruct your patient to lie on his or her back and ensure that he or she is comfortable and relaxed. Place one of the larger crystals at the patient's head with the single-terminated end pointing upwards. The other large quartz crystal should be placed at the feet with the single-terminated end facing upwards towards the body of the patient.

The remaining 10 quartz crystals are placed around the body; five on each side, with all their single-terminated ends facing upwards towards the patient's head; one opposite the ankles, one opposite the knees, one opposite the hands, one opposite the elbows and one opposite the shoulders; on both sides of the body.

A 13th, or control, quartz crystal (I usually use my selenite wand) – is then passed directly over the other 12 crystals, in a clockwise direction, to create a unified magnetic energy field around the patient.

The patient should lie in this position – cocooned in a 'sea' of healing energy – for between 15 and 20 minutes. This 12-crystal configuration is specially used for balancing and harmonising the whole body. While the patient is receiving the full benefit of these crystal healing energies I usually do a complete 'aura-scan' of the body. Starting at their head and placing my hands about six inches above their body I slowly move down the whole body using my hands as 'sensors'. Whenever I detect a possible

Crystal Triangulation (see page 128)

'imbalance' or negative blockage or energy blockage my hands start to become red hot!

Having made a mental note of where the blockages exist I then pass my control crystal in an anti-clockwise direction over the affected areas. This has the effect of clearing the blockage almost immediately and neutralising any negativity that may have existed.

In using the 12-crystal configuration I have found that all my patients have experienced a profound metamor-

115

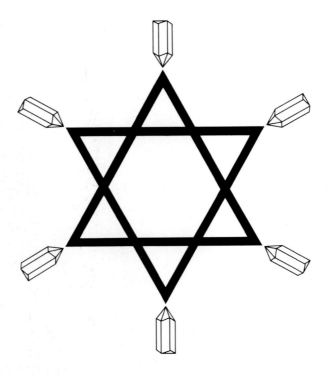

Figure 5. Star of David Configuration. The patient sits in the middle, in yoga fashion, holding a crystal in the palm of the hand.

phosis by the time their healing session has ended. An inner depth of peace and tranquillity is usually achieved and, at the right time, it is possible to trigger an emotional release of stress and tension, the power of which is almost imposs-ible to describe!

During all my workshops and seminars, when dem-onstrating the 12-crystal configuration, I ask for volunteers from among those present to receive this treatment. Usually the person who volunteers is exactly the right person on whom to demonstrate as I find that they are in urgent need of treatment. It is an interesting fact that a large percentage of people who attend my workshops and seminars do so because they have an inner desire to receive crystal healing for themselves as much as to learn how to use the various techniques which I am teaching and demonstrating.

The energy and power created in a typical workshop or seminar is truly remarkable and helps greatly when it comes to focusing the love and healing on the volunteer. Often the volunteer experiences a profound release of emotional tension, deep negative blockages are removed and a great change comes over them. Sometimes I have to give them additional healing and counselling, in private, afterwards, so that they are able to release all that they need to.

Crystal healing, through configurations, works upon all the subtle energy levels of the body and brings to the surface all the pent-up emotions and feelings of many years. In crystal healing treatments we seldom try to diagnose our patient's health condition in normal layman's – or even medical – terms. All dis-ease or ill health occurs through an imbalance of our normal level of bodily vibrations.

Using crystals and gemstones – whichever technique we choose – our main purpose is always to re-balance the imbalances of our patient's physical and mental bodies. No cures can be guaranteed. Indeed, it would be unprofessional and unethical for a natural health therapist to do so. But improvements can, and regularly do, occur. Although the medical profession, on the whole, regards us natural health practitioners as 'quacks', it is encouraging to note that more and more doctors are contacting us for information about

Twelve-crystal configuration (see page 114)

crystal healing. A few doctors are even using crystals in conjunction with their own allopathic medicine. Whatever the illness, from cancer to the common cold, crystal healing may help to improve the condition.

If the time and conditions are right healing may take place. However, we are all subject to the natural laws of karma (the law of cause and effect) and if we are meant to suffer for something we have done in a previous incarnation then all the positive healing in the world will not help.

Crystal healing can help people of all ages. People in their 70s and 80s often visit me, indignant and upset, because having lived very active lives, for the first time, perhaps ever, they are suffering from a severe illness which they find inconvenient.

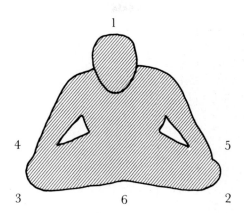

Figure 6. Star of David Configuration.

One elderly lady, in her mid-70s, hobbled into my healing room accompanied by her sister. She had been unable to walk properly for the previous 14 years. I helped her onto my massage couch and she lay down on her back. However, her left leg would not lie flat and she could only manage to have her knee arched up in the air.

I placed the 12 quartz crystals around her body and created a strong unified magnetic energy field around her with my control crystal. Within five minutes her left leg slowly began to move back down the table and lay flat on the couch. Her sister's mouth opened in astonishment.

By the time the healing session had finished, 20 minutes later, my patient was a completely different person. She walked out of my healing room in a way she would never have previously believed possible! She still telephones me from time to time and her leg continues to improve.

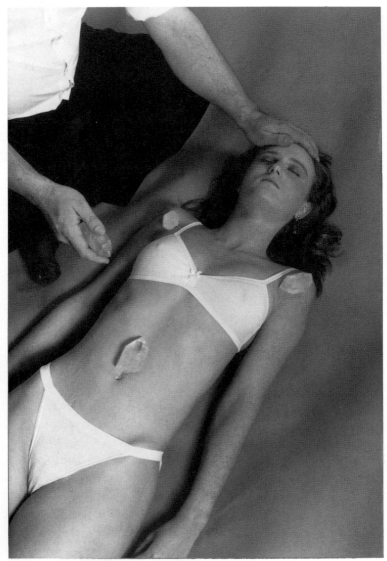

Crystal Triangulation on body above waist

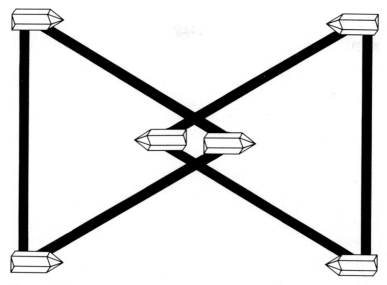

Figure 7. This is a crystal configuration which helps two individuals (lovers, spouses, good friends) to understand each other and to resolve any conflicts which might be present in their relationship.

The Star of David is another very effective type of crystal configuration. The patient should sit on the floor, in yoga fashion, holding a quartz crystal in the palm of her hand. Six quartz crystals should then be placed around her in the form of a six-pointed star.

The two major points of the configuration; 1 – behind the back and 2 – in front of the feet when the patient is sitting in the lotus position, symbolise the balancing point between the spiritual at the back and the physical at the front. These are the two crystals involved in the repolarisation and balance of vibrations within the patient.

The crystals on the sides, closest to the back, 4 and 5, are the other points relating to the spiritual trinity. The two crystals on the left side, 2 and 5, relate to the lower half of the body, from the waist down, both spiritually and physically. The two crystals on the right side, 3 and 4, relate to the upper half of the body, both spiritually and physically.

The Star of David crystal configuration enables you to cover all aspects of the patient's being and to correct the spiritual and physical energy flows throughout the body.

If the patient is suffering from any serious physical ailment then I suggest that you use your largest crystal in position 6, in the triangle relating to the physical. By doing this there will be a greater flow of energy to heal the physical vibrations. If the patient is in fairly good health, and the main purpose of the healing session is to treat spiritual or emotional stress then I advise placing your largest quartz crystal in position 1.

The seventh quartz crystal in the Star of David pattern is called the 'generator' and should be held in the hands of the person receiving the healing. It acts as the receiver of energies that will be dispersed to the six surrounding crystals, to unify the magnetic energy field and to allow the body to draw what it needs from the flow of energy.

Every crystal healer should acquire at least one 'generator' quartz which should be kept solely for that purpose. This 'generator' quartz crystal will gradually develop into an extension of their own energy pattern. It will become 'charged' with their energies and will become increasingly effective the more it is used.

The Star of David crystal configuration can also be used effectively with the patient lying on his or her back. One quartz crystal should be placed at the head with the single-terminated end pointing away from the body. Two quartz

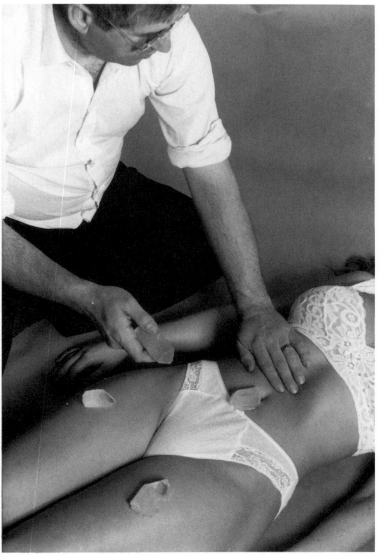

Crystal Configuration on body below waist

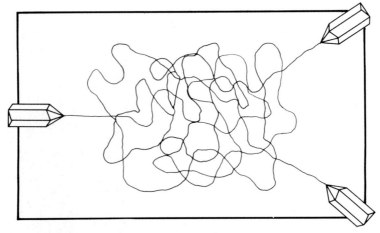

Figure 8. Bed patterns create an even flow of crystalline energy over the whole bed area which penetrates the body at all levels whilst one is asleep. (see page 129)

crystals should be placed at the knees, pointing upwards.

The crystal healer, as before, should take his personal healing crystal and energise the six crystals surrounding the patient's body by passing his crystal over all six quartz crystals several times. The patient should then lie within this healing field of crystalline energy for a further 15–20 minutes.

All disease and general ill-health, whether physical or mental, usually responds to crystal configurations to some degree and an improvement is normally self-evident after the first treatment.

For broken bones I suggest that you use two single-terminated quartz crystals. Place one below the fracture and one above the fracture with the points facing each other. This will speed up the healing process once the bones

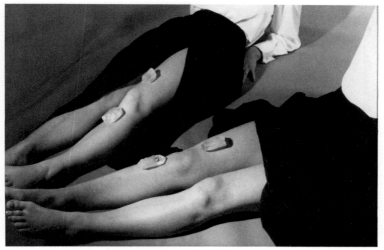

Treating fractures and sprains (see page 126)

have been set properly by a qualified doctor and will also decrease the chance of infection and complications.

The patient may also have a 12-figure crystal configuration placed around him or her at the same time. For burns you should use the same treatment as you would for broken bones. You may also hold a third quartz crystal over the burn area which will help to speed up the formation of new skin.

For hearing problems, use three single-terminated quartz crystals: one at the top of the head, pointing downwards, and the other two behind the ears in the mastoid area, pointing inwards.

For spinal disorders the patient should lie on the floor face downwards. Place a single-terminated quartz crystal between the ankles pointing upwards towards the base of the spine.

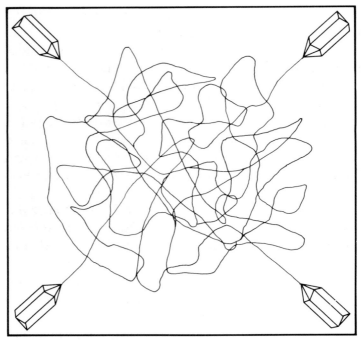

Figure 9. Room patterns create a room completely filled with pure vibrant crystalline energy (see page 130)

Place one crystal with the point downwards over the affected area of the spine. You do not want the energy to travel the whole length of the spine, only to the afflicted area.

For sprains in the ankle place a single quartz crystal on the foot, with the point on the ball of the foot. Hold another single quartz crystal, pointing downwards, at the knee. If the sprain is in the wrist, hold one crystal in the hand with the point upwards and the other at the shoulder with the point downwards. If the sprain is in the knee, place one crystal on the ball of the foot and the other crystal at the hip with the point downwards.

Migraine headaches are basically caused through the imbalance of energy flow throughout the physical body. To treat migraine successfully I would use four single-terminated quartz crystals; one on each side of the neck between the neck and the collar bone with all the points facing downwards. The two other quartz crystals should be positioned so as to lean against the balls of the feet with the point upwards. This will balance the energy flow through the main meridians.

There are many different types of crystal configurations and they can be used successfully to help sort out serious problems with relationships; whether that relationship is with a spouse, lover, or simply a friend. If two people are in conflict with each other, perhaps from stress or misunderstanding, I strongly recommend a pattern of double triangulation quartz crystals.

This pattern will help create an understanding between the two and thus serve to establish a sound balance between the flow of their vibrations. The two individuals should sit facing each other, approximately three feet apart, in the lotus position. Each person should take two quartz crystals and place them in a line behind themselves. They should then place a third quartz crystal in a position that forms a triangle with the other two crystals, in front of them, with the single-terminated end facing the other person.

Draw an imaginary line at the mid-point between the two people. The pointer crystal should be over that line, into the area of the other person. This will serve to interlock both triangles and form an invisible diamond in the centre where the two triangles intercept each other.

The effect you are creating is a symbolic one. You are taking the energies of the trinity of one, and blending them with the energies of the trinity of the other. The results will be both healing and releasing, and will create an understanding between the two.

This pattern of configuration is extremely effective when used between two individuals whose spiritual vibrations are closely aligned as it will unite them even closer. It could also be effective when used between a parent and a child, to create a more peaceful and understanding relationship between them.

*   *   *   *

In addition to these crystal configurations I also use various crystal triangulations. Triangulations use three quartz crystals to form a triangular concentration of crystalline energy either around the patient's body or in a specific area of the body.

For example, have your patient undress and lie on his or her back. To treat upper body health conditions, place two quartz crystals, one on each shoulder, with their points downwards and place a single crystal just below the navel with its point upwards. This will complete a 'triangulation' of crystalline energy pulsating throughout the upper part of the patient's body.

For lower body health conditions, place a single crystal, point downwards, just above the navel and two other quartz crystals, one on each thigh, points facing upwards. This will create a triangulation of crystalline energy concentrated upon the lower part of the patient's body.

You may wish to create your own crystal triangulations to meet the particular needs of the patient.

Crystal triangulations, with the patient sitting in a comfortable chair are also very powerful. For healing the physical body place one quartz crystal in front of the chair with the single-terminated end facing away from the patient and two quartz crystals, one on either side of the chair, and slightly behind it, with their crystal points facing towards the patient.

For healing of the spiritual part of the body, place one quartz crystal behind the chair, with its single-terminated end facing away from the patient and two other quartz crystals, one on either side, in front of the chair, with their crystal points directed towards the patient.

While the patient is sitting in the chair, within either of the above two triangulations, the crystal healer should pass his or her personal quartz crystal in a circular clockwise motion, over the patient and the three quartz crystals encompassing the chair, in order to create a unified magnetic crystal energy field surrounding the patient's body.

*   *   *   *

Bed patterns are a form of triangulation which establish an energy force field while the patient is asleep in bed at night. This triangulation creates a wonderful healing power and energy that builds resistance to all outside negativity and ensures a peaceful period of relaxation and repose.

To create a bed pattern the quartz crystals should be placed between the mattress and the bedsprings or simply placed on the floor under the bed. One crystal should be put at the top centre of the bed, with its single-terminated end facing inwards, the other two should be placed at the two corners of the opposite end of the bed. Each crystal point should be directed towards the centre of the bed.

This bed pattern creates a triangle of concentrated crystalline energy that will benefit anyone who lies within it. The field of crystal energy will gradually spread out until the entire bed becomes a powerful force field. Throughout the night, while the patient is asleep, these crystal energies gently penetrate all levels of the body helping to energise the whole being and improve general health and happiness.

Whenever you create your individual bed pattern, you must always be very clear in your mind what it is you wish to achieve through programming your bed pattern.

*　　*　　*　　*

Room patterns create an energy field which projects positive vibrations, removes all negativity and strengthens your energies every day. Place one quartz crystal in each corner of the room, the single-terminated end facing into the centre of the room. Each crystal may be placed on the floor or fixed to the ceiling.

The quartz crystals must be left in place at all times to have the maximum effect. You will soon find that they will generate a field of pure positive energy, allowing you to remain free of any unwanted negative energies that your clients, friends and visitors unconsciously emit.

As with bed patterns, whenever placing the quartz crystals to form a room pattern, it is important that you possess a clear idea of the prime purpose for which you have created the crystal energy field. This will ensure that you do not take on any negative or draining energy from those around you.

CHAPTER 12

The Total Healing Experience

The total healing experience involves bringing together a combination of crystals, colour and sound to make the perfect trinity. All dis-ease and ill health arises out of an imbalance in our bodily vibrations. If we can formulate a 'package' of healing techniques that includes crystal, colour and sound we should, in theory, be able to provide virtually instantaneous healing.

Of course we are all subject to the laws of karma, which must be taken into consideration, and sometimes it may not be appropriate or 'right' for every patient to automatically be cured by receiving a single healing treatment.

Colour healing and sound therapy, like crystal healing, also work on the principle of re-balancing bodily vibrations. They, therefore, have much in common with the way in which we work with crystals.

At present we have researchers investigating colour therapy, experimenting with the effects of sound therapy and, of course, others like myself who are discovering 'new' crystal healing techniques. In the fullness of time I believe that all three areas will begin to merge into one cohesive unit.

It is known that the healing priests in the ancient continent of Atlantis were knowledgeable in the use of crystals, colour and sound energies for healing purposes. We must allow our souls to become more receptive so that not only may we begin to rediscover this long forgotten wisdom and understanding but also so that we may use these ancient truths to the benefit of mankind.

Very simply, each chakra vibrates on a different colour frequency, thus:

The Base Chakra	= red
The Sexual Chakra	= orange
The Solar Plexus Chakra	= yellow
The Heart Chakra	= green
The Throat Chakra	= blue
The Brow Chakra	= indigo
The Crown Chakra	= violet

and, each colour vibrates on a different sound frequency, thus

Red	= F sharp
Orange	= B flat
Yellow	= G major
Green	= C and E combined
Blue	= D sharp
Indigo	= A minor
Violet	= B, D and G combined

Use of the right combination, in conjunction with the appropriate crystal healing configuration, should, in theory, bring about instantaneous healing.

All the quartz crystals used in any configuration should be bathed in the colour associated with the area of the disease and, by evoking the vibrations of the relevant sound or note at the same time, a complete harmony of vibrations will be created that is totally compatible with the organic structure of the body.

Some researchers in the field of complementary medicine have been experimenting for many years with the effects of colour and colour therapy upon the human body. The same researchers are now also beginning to investigate sound therapy.

I believe that we are fast approaching a time when we shall be able to expand our crystal consciousness and knowledge, here in the 20th century, in a way that few people have dared to dream so far.

The days of Atlantis may be long gone but the Atlanteans left behind them technical data and information that is far in advance of anything that our 20th century scientists can offer.

Atlantis disintegrated because cosmic power and universal laws were being abused and misused for selfish and bestial purposes. All power, it is said, corrupts, and so it was in those darkest days of Atlantis. Some of the priests who were in charge of the largest Atlantean generator crystals wanted increasing power for themselves. They wanted total power and dominance over all the people that dwelt in Atlantis and they worked very hard to enslave everybody and make them subservient to them! It was fortunate, however, that not all the priests in Atlantis were corrupt. Some of the priests and priestesses were able to retain their integrity and wisdom.

These priests 'programmed' special quartz crystals known as 'record keeper' crystals and 'laser wand' crystals with all the blue-prints and scientific technology known to the Atlanteans. This was to ensure that this important data and information would be available to future generations when the conditions were absolutely 'right' and when the 'right' people would come along who could be entrusted with this sacred knowledge.

This sacred knowledge has been mostly inaccessible until now. Some of the record keeper crystals and laser wands have been rediscovered and it can only be a matter of time before the perfect conditions are created whereby the secrets of the ancient continent of Atlantis will once more be revealed. When this happens we shall all receive a profound cultural shock.

Already, a few people have been able to decode some of the information hidden within these record keeper crystals. But the information so far obtained has barely scratched the surface! Obtaining all the information from our record keepers will prove to be a long task but the wait will, I am sure, be very worthwhile. We must all, however, accept personal responsibility for ensuring that our planet does not become a second Atlantis! We must ensure that, once the secrets of the record keeper crystals have been revealed, we do not allow this knowledge to be misused again.

The Atlantean priests, who had the task of 'programming' the record keeper crystals and laser wands before the final destruction of Atlantis, foresaw the dangers of making their sacred knowledge available to the wrong people. They knew that if this knowledge should fall into the wrong hands then that would once again be the end of civilisation as we know it.

When you have finished reading this book you must accept personal responsibility to use the information contained here for the benefit of mankind, and not for personal gain.

CHAPTER 13

Colour Crystal Healing

For all my colour crystal healing treatments I have designed my own special crystal light box. It is a rectangular or square box with a hole in the centre in which a small light bulb is placed.

Colour filters are placed over the hole where the light shines up through the box. Crystal light box quartz crystals are placed over the filters. When quartz crystals are used in this way those colour rays that may be used for healing and upliftment are intensified and projected into the environment.

Light box crystals can be either flat based, single generator crystals or clusters. The main requirement for a light box crystal is the ability to reflect light from the base up through the entire crystal.

After a crystal has been used on the light box with one colour, and you wish to use it with another colour, it is best to cleanse the crystal first.

For many thousands of years colour and colour rays have been used for healing purposes. Colour impinges on our every waking moment and even penetrates our dreams. All around us, everything we use, wear and see is coloured. So, what is colour?

Many people have quite definite ideas and feelings about colour. The love of colour springs from the individual's inner consciousness. Colour affects us emotionally, making things warm or cold, provocative or sympathetic, exciting or tranquil. Some people are more sensitive to colour than others. While some are attracted, even fascinated by certain colours others may be repelled or seem quite unaffected by the same colour vibrations.

It is, therefore, apparent that colour exerts a powerful influence upon our minds and emotions. Colour is not a lifeless, static phenomenon, as many people suppose, but a vital force, a strong influence on all our lives. Colour is an important tool, though few people see it as such, or think about how it may be 'managed'. Colour consultants 'manage' colour when they are able to awaken interest and increase productivity with a thoughtful colour scheme for a factory or office; create moods with restaurant lighting schemes or make quiet diesel locomotives more visible at level crossings.

Colour management can include designing sleep-inducing colour schemes for bedrooms, or dressing children in colours that stand out against dull streets thereby reducing the risk of accidents. Some psychologists can even analyse individuals from the way they choose and use colour.

Colour is an interface between us and the world, although insufficient education in colour makes most people's handling of it something of a hit-and-miss affair. Many people use colour impressively in their dress, yet their homes may indicate neither taste nor courage because they do not understand colour. People dress once or twice a day but decorate, on average, bi-annually. Yet it is the colour around them that most affects their moods and personality.

Knowledge, judgement and intuition, are all combined in the capable management of colour which is a discipline and an art. Among the many rewards of its mastery are a greater sensitivity to the medium of colour and increased satisfaction from its handling. Knowing how colours are named and standardised, how they change under different kinds of lighting, why they fade, and how they can be used to alter mood, line, form, shape and perspective, understanding the optical effects of certain colour combinations and the psychological impact of coloured lighting – all are essential if you are to succeed in making colour do what you want it to do!

There is an ancient and widespread faith in the healing power of colour and a belief that this power can be used to heal imbalances of both the mind and body. Imagine how great this power must be when combined with the might and energy of the quartz crystal?

Gemstones, seemingly filled with coloured light of a peculiarly mystical kind, have always been held in reverence and in ancient times were ground and diluted, or dipped in water, to be used as remedies for all diseases. Yellow beryls, for example, were used to cure jaundice; bloodstones treated haemorrhages and disorders of the blood and the prismatic diamond was considered a cure-all, as is the quartz crystal today.

Only about 100 years ago, the association of colour and therapy, crystals and therapy, and certainly the combination of colour, crystals and therapy was considered by most conventional doctors to be in the realms of quackery.

The theories of the majority of colour/crystal therapists are based on the aura, the emanations which many psychics claim surrounds the human body.

Perfect health of the body and mind depend on a balance of aural colours, and a balance of the inner centres of vital force – the chakras. Should a colour be missing or over dominant, the balance must be redressed by colour crystal healing.

Man has been colour conscious since the beginning of time. Colour laws and teachings were always present in the wisdom teachings of the prophets.

The famous psychic, Edgar Cayce, often spoke in trance about some of his patients having existed 'in Atlantean land – during the time when there was the creating of a high influence of radial activity from rays of the sun that were turned on crystals in the pits that made connections with internal influences of the earth'.

Cayce also speaks of 'machines used for obtaining power from the crystals' and he mentions those who were 'among those that interpreted the messages received through the crystals' and indicates that there were temples of healing in Atlantis similar to those constructed in Egypt.

In these temples of healing, the forces of colour and crystals were always used, not only to assist in worship, but also as an aid to healing. These temples would have been orientated so that the sun shone through the dome-shaped roof in such a way that its light was broken up into seven prismatic colours, and the sick were bathed in their special colour, necessary at that time to restore their health. The Egyptians assigned colours to the body; red to the physical body, yellow to the astro-mental and blue to the spiritual. It would seem, therefore, that humans have had a similar reaction to colour for thousands of years!

Colour exists on all planes of life, as vibrations are everywhere and colour is a manifestation of vibration. The sun, the universal light, emanates vibratory streams of life force in seven major rays.

Each individual is believed to incarnate into their own specific colour, which is the major ray, and this contains their very own individual shade of degree of evolution. Everybody also possesses three other rays, known as the minor rays, which are the soul colours. When all these rays are in harmony the individual will enjoy good health and abundant energy. When the rays are not in harmony, however, energy levels will decrease and sickness will occur. It is at this time that the living energy of both colour and crystals can be used to create, restore and renew. Every colour has positive and negative tones. Clear, strong tones of a colour in the aura indicate the positive qualities: application, force and will. Weak, faded or dull tones in the aura indicate lack of force and instability. Some colours are warming: red, orange and yellow, some are cooling: blue, violet and magenta; while green, the middle or balancing colour, is neutral.

The more light that a person attracts, through spiritual living and high ideals, the more beautiful will be the colours of their aura. The highly evolved person will have only positive tones, properly balanced and controlled. They will appear to be surrounded by rays of light which will be soothing and healing to others.

In the aura of the less evolved person, the colours will be less pure and less luminous. The auric colours may be clouded, dull and unpleasant to see – there may be 'clouds', 'flecks' or even 'holes' in the aura, and one can usually intuitively tell if the reasons for these imbalances are due to stress, illness, weakness, the taking of drugs, alcohol, smoking, or poor nutrition. Colour and crystals can be used in all healing, as a universal therapeutic tool, upon all levels of metaphysical existence.

The seven major chakras, or energy centres, are all 'keyed' to the seven colours of the spectrum.

The sacral, or base, chakra affects the gonads and is associated with the colour red. The adrenal, or splenic chakra, affects the adrenal glands and is associated with the colour orange.

The solar plexus chakra is symbolised by the colour yellow and governs everything to do with the mind and concentration. The heart chakra is associated with the colours green and pink and affects one's emotional relationships.

The throat chakra is represented by the colour blue and affects the thyroid. The brow, or third eye, chakra is associated with the colour violet or purple and affects the pituitary gland while the crown chakra represents the pineal gland and is associated with the colour magenta or indigo.

Imbalances in any one chakra or several chakras will affect the whole being. Healing can be effected in many different ways, but there are two principal methods of applying colour crystal therapy: either by the application of colour to a part of, or the whole of, the body, with beams of light shone through coloured filters and magnified by the use of a light box quartz crystal; or by the use of gemstones according to their individual colours.

The first method requires the acquisition of a crystal

light box. These can be obtained from Crystal 2000 or, if you prefer, you can construct your own.

The most practical form of light box is one that is small and easily portable. The bulb should be a full spectrum daylight blue, giving the same effect as natural daylight, and on no account should you ever use an ultra-violet bulb. The light box should be constructed so that the light is reflected through the opening, which can be either at the front or on top of the light box.

It is very important that your light box should be made in such a way that the filters can be changed quietly and easily without disturbing the patient or burning the therapist. It should also be properly ventilated so that no undue heat is felt by the patient; the object of the exercise is light, not heat! Treatment will be made much easier if the light box can be mounted on a stand so that it can be easily tilted to various angles, or raised or lowered.

The most important part of the crystal light box is the filters and, if possible, only hand-crafted stained glass should be used. This will have a density and vibration which cannot be manufactured artificially and, like any natural material from mother earth, can be cleansed and dedicated for your particular purpose and all traces of negativity removed. The glow of stained glass is as much the result of bubbles and impurities as anything else; the light is not just admitted, but held, giving a luminous, 'jewel-like', quality.

Each filter made from hand-crafted stained glass, no matter what colour it appears to be, will contain the entire spectrum of colours within it and its properties are truly magical. The glaziers working with stained glass today are visionary artists on a grand scale; their raw material is daylight, the visible manifestation of God in creation, which they can translate with glass into vibrant colour.

Only five basic colours need be obtained – red, yellow, green, violet and blue – as the following colours can be created from these combinations:

Red and yellow	= orange
Blue and violet	= indigo
Yellow and green	= lemon
Blue and green	= turquoise
Red and violet	= magenta
Blue and Red	= scarlet

For general colour crystal healing treatments, I recommend that you use an almost transparent quartz crystal. The crystal should be placed on top of the coloured filter so that the light can be projected towards the patient. As the light shines through the coloured filter it makes the crystal glow with the colour of the filter you have used.

It is best to keep one special light box quartz crystal for all colour crystal healing treatments and the crystal should always be cleansed between patients.

The decision of which colour filter to choose for the treatment session will be depend largely on your own observation of the patient and his symptoms. Never, however, underestimate your own intuitive faculties as often your intuition is the most reliable guide you possess.

You will probably have discovered that one or more of the chakra centres is out of balance and you will need to treat the most appropriate chakra or chakras in order to restore harmony to the body.

The following is a guide to the application of some of the colours:

Red

This is the most powerful, and should, therefore, be used carefully and wisely. It is revitalising, stimulating and arousing; it promotes inhalation and raises the blood pressure. It can be useful in treating chronic diseases, and helps with rheumatism and arthritis.

Orange

This is an anti-depressant, promotes good digestion, and is beneficial to most of the metabolic system; it increases oxygen and so helps the lungs function properly. It can draw boils and bring abscesses to a head. It is rejuvenating, but can also raise blood pressure.

Yellow

Can stimulate the nervous system, helps with mental illness and stimulates the lymphatic glands. It may help with the treatment of arthritis by removing density deposits in the body.

Green

Like red, green must be used carefully. Although it is the ray of balance, overuse can promote the dissolving of virgin cell structure, as well as the inverted cells. It stimulates the pituitary, raises the vibrations, and is very beneficial for minor cuts, sores and bruises. It is the colour to use in the treatment of cancer, but it must never be used on pregnant women.

Turquoise

Refreshing and cooling, turquoise is restful for a nervous patient and also helps treat inflammation. It is also good for eczema.

Blue

Of all the colours blue is the most healing. It promotes exhalation and reduces blood pressure. It is the light of peace, relaxing the whole body and regulating the harmonious development of tissue and body structure. Blue removes headaches and migraines, and is useful in cases of asthma. It aids sleep, reduces fear, soothes infections and inflammations and relieves itches and burns.

Violet

In this colour two effects are combined; the relaxing in the blue and the stimulating in the red. It is the colour of a consciousness balance – the colour of divinity, creativity and also stability. It will raise the self-esteem of an individual who has lost the sense of human beauty and restore rhythm to the system.

Magenta

This colour draws the patient into spiritual awareness. It should be used only rarely and is usually a colour for the more mature person.

It is also important to remember that each colour also has an emotional and mental quality which should be taken into account when treating your patient as the psychological condition often affects the physical.

Red   = energy
Orange   = joy
Yellow   = detachment
Green   = balance/equilibrium
Turquoise = immunity
Blue   = relaxing
Violet   = dignity/self-respect
Magenta   = dissolving/letting go

One very important colour which has not yet been mentioned is pink; the colour usually associated with love, the emotions and, particularly, with mother-love. The colour pink has a calming effect on the emotional level and helps people suffering from emotional trauma or problems with their relationships.

Another method used in colour crystal healing is the use of polished gemstones. Gemstones are used by some healers in colour crystal healing treatments because they are pure in colour, unmixed and unadulterated in their effect and the rays are concentrated within the gemstones themselves.

One theory accounting for their effectiveness is that the planets influence human behaviour physically, psychologically, emotionally and spiritually and since the gemstones possess the same rays as the planets, they exert the same influence, albeit less forcefully, as the planets.

The true colour of a gemstone is revealed by the use of the prism. For example, the rays of a diamond are seen as white by the naked eye, but are indigo when seen under the prism. Therefore, indigo is the true colour of the diamond.

The use of gemstones according to their particular colours can, on occasions, be a little confusing, as many gemstones have healing properties which do not appear to correspond with the colour of that particular centre in the body!

Although I may recommend that a patient wears or carries a particular stone around with them, my suggestion may have been made on the basis of its colour or, alternatively, for its inherent healing properties and in some cases they may not match.

Take some of the green stones, for example. The emerald is said to improve the intellect and memory and help cure insomnia. Malachite helps treat asthma, toothache, irregular periods and improves eyesight. Peridot aids indigestion, heals hurt feelings, helps bruised eyes and repairs damaged relationships. Jade is mainly used for kidney complaints and bladder trouble. Aventurine is generally thought to be good for skin diseases and improves vitality. But perhaps the key to the problem is more subtle; all the symptoms listed above are purely physical manifestations of an imbalance within the soul. So look carefully at your patient, and try to determine why they are manifesting a damaged kidney or skin rash. What is the psychological cause for it? If, for example, the indication for treatment is a gemstone which happens to be green, look at what is happening in the patient's heart chakra! My advice at all times is to use your intuition whenever you are not sure what to do.

Colour crystal healing may either be used as a therapy in its own right or in conjunction with another major therapy (e.g. acupuncture).

During the past few years I have distributed crystal light boxes to therapists representing all the major natural health therapies and the number is increasing. A colour crystal healing therapist once told me that whenever he is feeling lethargic he places a yellow filter on his crystal light box for 15 minutes. He says that this short treatment provides him with sufficient energy to work half the night! Colour crystal healing is undoubtedly a powerful therapeutic healing tool, which can be used by therapists anywhere, at any time, to bring help and relief to those within their care. It is yet another example of ancient wisdom being recognised in the 20th century.

Chapter 14

Gem Elixirs

For information on gem elixirs I am indebted to my friend and colleague, Frank Eastwood.

Gem elixirs are liquid preparations made from gem stones. They are prepared by placing the stones in a clear class bowl of water. Leave the bowl in sunlight for several hours. The water that has been 'charged' by the gemstone can then be filtered off and preserved with alcohol.

The term 'gem elixir' covers the use of any material of mineral origin and is not just confined only to semi-precious or precious gemstones. It includes the use of elements extracted from minerals by man as well as certain materials, such as amber or petrified wood, which could be classified as being of vegetable origin. Thus, one of my gem elixirs has been prepared from amber and another from metallic aluminium.

Gem elixirs are very helpful for the treatment of problems arising from negative emotions and thoughts. The dosage used is 10 drops twice a day for one month. If necessary the dosage can be repeated more frequently, for example, five drops four times a day.

Gem elixirs can be used undiluted, or diluted with still spring water and preserved with a little brandy. Whether the elixirs are used diluted or undiluted depends upon the individual. Usually the patient benefits most from the undiluted elixir for the first month followed by a dilution of, say, four drops to 10ml. However, this can be adjusted for each individual. The length of treatment can be several months and you may have to change the elixirs monthly although the patient usually makes quite considerable progress in one month. For example, after treatment for a negative aspect of an emotional problem treatment that will enhance a positive aspect of the same or a different emotion is required.

The electromagnetic vibration of the stone is transferred to the water during the preparation of the gem elixir. When the elixir is taken by the patient these electromagnetic properties are assimilated into the chakras thus rectifying any imbalance.

Gem elixirs can be used in conjunction with other forms of treatment without interfering with that treatment. Any practitioner who does not use crystal therapy will find that gem elixirs are very useful.

Homoeopathic practitioners will find gem elixirs particularly useful as the treatments complement each other and work well together. For example, gem elixirs are useful after acupuncture. The right elixir will prevent a recurrence of the emotional disturbance which necessitated the acupuncture treatment. Usually two gem elixirs are used, one for the most over-energised meridian and one for the most under-energised. Gem elixirs are also very useful for treating chakra imbalances. In this case one or two gem elixirs, sometimes three, would be needed.

I recommend gem elixirs only for the treatment of psychological or emotional problems, never for physical disorders. This is because, in the United Kingdom, gem elixirs are outside The Medicines Act. Any product which makes claims for the treatment of physical ailments has to have a product licence and have undergone clinical trials. It is illegal to advertise gem elixirs as a cure for specific diseases unless a product licence has been granted for such a claim.

I have used many methods to determine the effectiveness of gem elixirs, including dowsing, electroacupuncture testing, applied kinesiology and the use of a psychological test.

Electroacupuncture is a diagnostic method which measures subtle energies in the body by means of electronic measuring equipment. The instrument I use is the Doctor Reckeweg Electroacupuncture Apparatus. This enables one to measure specific acupuncture points on the body or the ear and can also be used to determine the state of the chakras and the subtle bodies, using homoeopathic test ampoules. It also enables one to determine which gem elixirs are effective in any given condition.

Applied Kinesiology is a system which evaluates the structural, chemical and mental aspects of a person. It employs standard muscle testing as well as other methods of diagnosis. Nutrition, manipulation and acupressure are used therapeutically to help restore well being. Muscle testing can be used to help evaluate the potential usefulness of gem elixirs.

My research has shown how gem elixirs relate to

the different components of the human aura, the electro-magnetic field surrounding the body.

Esoteric philosophy considers that man has several different types of body:

1) The physical body.

2) The etheric body – the framework on which the physical body is constructed.

The etheric body transmits energy to the physical body. There are seven chakras or energy centres in the etheric body plus the spleen chakra that obtains and circulates energy to the physical body. The chakras are defined as biophysical resonators that activate the endocrine glands and maintain the health of the organ systems. The seven major spinal chakras are involved with various levels of consciousness.

3) The emotional body – this is where we experience the joys and sadnesses of life. The ovoid shaped emotional body exists approximately 15 inches from the physical body. There are seven chakras associated with this body.

4) The mental body – this comprises the lower concrete mind, which is logic derived from knowledge, and the higher abstract mind, where intuitive faculties are exercised and pure reason occurs. Seven chakras are associated with the mental body.

5) The soul, consisting of three parts:

a) The monad, which directs the life of the person.

b) The atmic body, which is associated with the will to live.

c) The buddhic body, which provides communication with universal intelligence.

Under- or over-activity of a chakra can sometimes occur. This happens because there is either too little or too much electro-magnetic energy within the chakra. Under- or over-activity of a chakra can lead to disease. It is equally true, however, that under- or over-active chakras can be found in an apparently healthy person, but you will probably find that the person has the negative emotions or thoughts that are associated with these chakra imbalances. Very rarely are all of the major chakras over- or under-active. Seriously ill people often have all seven chakras plus the spleen chakra under-active. Usually two or three chakras are out of balance.

How do chakras become unbalanced? By the wrong use of emotional energy, by the wrong use of thought patterns, by upbringing or by other factors.

Gem elixirs provide an excellent means of regulating chakra imbalances. Each elixir is specific to a particular chakra and its possible imbalances so you should choose two or three gem elixirs to balance the chakras and restore them to normal activity.

The descriptions of my own 50 gem elixirs are included below. These descriptions should only be used as a general guide for prescribing and not as a substitute for actual measurements of acupuncture meridian or chakra imbalances.

The main difficulty in using the following descriptions is that a patient is unlikely to admit to, for example, being cruel, vindictive and full of hatred. However, the practitioner is able to reach that conclusion from the chakra or acupuncture meridian imbalances because of known psychological states that are related to these particular imbalances. Also these descriptions are useful to the practitioner because it is possible to deduce these by giving a psychological test.

Indications for the use of gem elixirs

Abalone: For those who have excessive anxiety and fear of others.

Blue Lace Agate: For hatred of others and suspicion.

Aluminium: For fear of emotional expression.

Amazonite: For help with social inadequacy.

Amber: For those in despair who need relief of some sort.

Amethyst: For those who strongly resist any interference with the freedom to make their own decisions and plans.

Aquamarine: For over-enthusiasm, tenseness, stress and strain.

Aragonite: For overcoming a feeling of helplessness.

Aventurine: For mental rigidity, high-mindedness, pride and aloofness.

Azurite: For those unable to control their own reality.

Beryl: For low self-esteem.

Black Onyx: For those unable to confront their emotions. For frustration with the slow development of events.

Black Tourmaline: For restlessness through a need to be more causative.

Bloodstone: For those who demand unquestioning affection.

Calcite: For feelings of emotional confinement. For the fear that there is no point in formulating fresh goals.

Chrysocolla: For those stuck in an over-organised life routine.

Chrysoprase: For arrogance and egotism.

Crocidolite: For those preoccupied with personal limitations.

Dolomite: For lack of resourcefulness or fear of failure.

Dioptase: For those who deny themselves emotionally.

Green Tourmaline: For those who set themselves idealistic but illusory goals with resulting disappointment.

Grossuralite: For fear of emotional hostility from others.

Hematite: For feelings of defencelessness.

Herkimer Diamond: For inability to achieve goals.

Jade: For those who require help in being realistic about their ideals.

Labradorite: For tension arising from frustration. For those whose relationships rarely meet expectations.

Magnesite: For emotional insecurity. For disappointment at the non-fulfilment of hopes.

Mahogany Obsidian: For those seeking an unrealistic perfection in their sex life.

Malachite: For those striving too hard to control their reality.

Moldavite: For inability to make decisions, lack of confidence.

Moonstone: For those who feel threatened by their environment. For the reckless spending of money.

Moss Agate: For repressed sexual feelings.

Nephrite: For those overwhelmed by details and pulled in many directions at once.

Opal: For suppressed agitation from attempting to resist any form of stimulation.

Pearl: For emotional excitement associated with fear.

Pink Tourmaline: For lack of creativity through a repressed personality.

Quartz: For protection against adverse environmental influences.

Rose Quartz: For lack of self-discipline or fear of responsibility.

Rutilated Quartz: For those who over-emphasise sensuous luxury.

Smoky Quartz: For fear of emotional interaction with others.

Rhodocrosite: For exhaustion arising from frustration.

Rhodonite: For physical exhaustion. For fear of criticism.

Selenite: For guilt and inability to relinquish the past. For those who are over-imaginative and given to fantasy.

Sodalite: For overcoming a desire for inappropriate action. For rage and a need for negative attention.

Staurolite: For over caution and doubt.

Thulite: For those resisting a condition or relationship regarded as discouraging.

Tiger's Eye: For those who are afraid of success.

Topaz: For those avoiding making a decision which would commit one to a course of action. For loss of willpower through lack of ability to make decisions.

Turquoise: For anxiety aggravated by darkness. For those who are seeking a way out of a problem but feel that there is no solution.

Watermelon Tourmaline: For a tendency to believe that which is still only an idea is already real.

Finally, the table below lists the various constituent parts of the anatomy discussed previously and describes which treatments are helpful for the individual parts of the anatomy. The purpose of this table is to show how gem elixirs relate to other treatment procedures.

The treatments shown in italics indicate that the treatment is particularly appropriate for that part of the body thus, for example, colour therapy is possibly the most appropriate treatment for the etheric and gem elixirs for the mental body.

Model of the Anatomy of Man

CONSTITUENT PART	TREATMENT REQUIRED
The soul	*Flower essences*
The mind	*Homoeopathy* – High potency 10m
Mental body & chakras	*Gem elixirs*, Flower essences
Emotional body & chakras	Gem elixirs, Flower essences
Etheric body & chakras	*Colour*, Gem elixirs, Flower essences
Acupuncture meridians	Herbs, Homoeopathy, Flower essences, Gem elixirs.
Physical body	Manipulation, Nutrition, Herbs, Acupuncture, Homoeopathy

I hope this brief introduction to gem elixirs has given

you an insight into how they are used, for what purposes and how they relate to other forms of treatment.

For further information about gem elixirs contact:

Frank Eastwood
39 Browns Lane
Coventry
West Midlands CV5 9DT
England
Telephone – 01203 403818

CHAPTER 15

The Bermuda Triangle

The Bermuda Triangle is situated in the middle of an area of the Atlantic ocean that once contained the continent of Atlantis.

Throughout the ages, since Atlantis was destroyed and sank beneath the waves, many seemingly inexplicable disappearances have occurred within the Bermuda triangle.

These disappearances, in my opinion, are the result of a powerful build up of energy from damaged fire crystals from Atlantis. Each fire crystal would have been at least 20 foot tall and eight foot wide. Originally they would have been erected in a series of three which would have created tremendous energy and power. When the force field emitted by these fire crystals becomes strong enough, anything entering the force field disintegrates and is transformed into pure energy.

The energy from these fire crystals exists all the time, but only at certain periods is the force powerful enough to effect this disintegration. There have been theories that many of the planes and ships lost within the Bermuda

Triangle have been jettisoned into some kind of black hole or time warp. This is not true. Those who have been caught up within this force field have simply been returned to spirit.

There have been occasions when ships that had vanished in the Bermuda Triangle have returned. The crew members, however, appeared to be insane, incoherent and relating wild stories. This is because at certain times when the force field from the fire crystals is not powerful enough to bring about total destruction it effects injuries instead. It is similar to someone receiving an overdose from a shock treatment to the brain. Not enough to kill the person, but enough to damage the brain structure and to cause insanity.

The babblings that these crew members relate are hallucinations and the indescribable horrors with which their minds cannot cope. Hence the reason they become insane.

CHAPTER 16

Pot-Pourri

* Amethysts were always popular in the ancient civilisations around the Mediterranean. Beautiful beads, exquisitely carved from amethyst, were found as early as the first dynasty in Egypt; some 5000 years ago.

There is a legend surrounding the origin of the name amethyst which explains its connection with modesty and how it came to be a purplish colour. According to the legend, Bacchus, the God of wine, had been slighted, and vowed to take his revenge on the first person to come along. So he ordered his tigers to eat whoever should happen to walk by.

Fate dictated that a maiden named Amethyst was on her way to worship at the temple of Diana, a goddess associated with modesty, when the tigers attacked her. The girl appealed to Diana for help and in a second the goddess had turned her devotee into a statue of clear crystal. Seeing this, Bacchus regretted his anger and poured a cup of wine over the crystal statue, thus creating a rich purple-hued stone.

* Take a piece of rose quartz – about 2lbs in weight – and twist, fairly tightly, a length of copper wire around the rose quartz leaving at least six inches free at each end. Place the rose quartz in front of you and take hold of both ends of the copper wire, a piece in each hand. Now relax. Quieten your mind and be still. After a few moments you will begin to feel a gentle pulsation within your hands. This energy will steadily increase and become very pleasant and euphoric. You will experience a deep sense of elation and a wonderful inner joy.

* Practice yoga or meditation for at least one hour. Then lie on your back and place a quartz crystal upon the middle of your third eye. Relaxation will occur and the mind become receptive. The subtle vibrations emanating from within the crystal will be strongly felt. Ask the crystal to reflect the answers from the truth within; and into your conscious awareness. Then allow your mind to open up to receive your answer which may come in symbols, images, visions or direct knowing.

* Quartz crystals are especially attractive to children, who seem to appreciate their beauty. A crystal hanging in a child's bedroom can become an endless source of fascination and delight.

* Crystals or gemstones may be placed under your pillow while you are asleep to help inspire lofty or prophetic dreams.

* Hanging a quartz crystal in a sunny window will act as a prism, filling the room with brilliant spectrums and adding colour and light to your surroundings. If the crystal is set gently in motion the room will sparkle as rainbows dance across the walls, floors and ceiling.

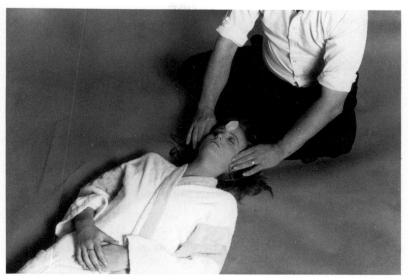

Crystal relaxation

* Quartz crystals have many interesting qualities apart from their visual attractiveness.

Quartz can produce an electric current when subjected to tension or pressure, and when it is influenced by an electric field it will vibrate rapidly at frequencies measured in millions per second. This is why quartz is used in resonators and oscillators for frequency control in electronic communications equipment.

* Granite usually contains between 20–40 per cent of quartz.

* Quartz crystals have the ability to transmit and amplify electromagnetic energy. For this reason, quartz is used extensively in the field of electronics. It can also be used to tune into the deeper, invisible parts of oneself, for

example, your thoughts, aura etc, as these are electromagnetic energy.

It is not essential for you to believe, or understand, the power of quartz crystals in order for them to help you, but if you can make an effort to work with your crystal, you can receive many benefits.

Hold your crystal as often as possible. The warmth of your body heats the crystal and excites the molecules, thereby intensifying its effectiveness. You can also carry your crystal in your pocket or purse. Some people sleep with their crystal under their pillow or in their hands. When you are not using your crystal, leave it on any surface in your home and it will generate energy for you.

* Once you have programmed your quartz crystals for a specific purpose (for example, meditation) it is best that you use your crystal for that purpose only.

If you do have to use a quartz crystal, which you have already programmed for another purpose, make certain that you project the thought into the crystal before you begin using it so that it will retain the programme that has already been placed within it.

You will soon discover, as you begin to use your crystals and gemstones with increased frequency, that if you are not clear yourself as to your purpose beforehand you will almost certainly discover the correct answers during the time that you are working with your crystals.

* Hold the terminated point of a clear quartz crystal up to your third eye chakra and visualise yourself as being calm, secure and confident. Project this thought form into your quartz crystal and then sit down quietly, holding the quartz crystal, as you mentally reaffirm to yourself the positive reality which you have now created.

If you need an answer to a specific question, ask it mentally and then placing your clear, single-terminated quartz crystal to your third eye chakra, visualise the solution within your mind's eye.

If you need to send loving thoughts and prayers to another person, place your quartz crystal pointing from your heart chakra and visualise the desired result as strongly as you can by projecting the image through your crystal to be received by the person for whom you are praying.

* The inhabitants of Atlantis used quartz crystals to channel and harness cosmic forces.

The Atlantean civilisation was so technologically advanced that the priests and priestesses could use crystals as beacons of light to serve as telepathic communicators to their universal forefathers.

Before Atlantis was destroyed the priests and priestesses wanted to preserve all the knowledge that they possessed for the benefit of generations to come. They dare not transcribe this data into books or manuscripts for fear that their records, knowledge and wisdom would either be totally lost when Atlantis was destroyed or that their records would fall into the wrong hands and their knowledge and wisdom once again misused.

They decided, therefore, to programme some of their quartz crystals and laser wands with all their scientific data, technology and information. These special crystals and laser wands were then de-materialised until the time was right for them to reappear. That time is now. They trusted that when the time was right these special crystals and laser wands would re-surface and once again be attracted to the

Crystal water

people who could attune their minds to receive the knowledge and wisdom stored within these crystals.

We call these crystals 'record keepers'.

* Try the following experiment when you next have 'flu:

Hold your personal quartz crystal and visualise yellow light radiating through it. Then place your crystal in water and drink this water the next day; take one cup of water at two-hourly intervals. You will be amazed at the results!

* Many of us experience the problem of hard tap water. One solution is to place a quartz crystal in a large jug of water, leave for a couple of hours, and then drink a glass of this water instead of your usual tap water. You will soon begin to appreciate the sparkling purity of your new crystal water.

* Anything Shirley Can Do:-

Shirley MacLaine, the film star, places quartz crystal clusters on the four corners of her bath every time she takes a bath or shower. Sounds like a great idea for reaching parts that other crystals can't reach. Try it for yourself – it's wonderful!

* Try this experiment – you will be amazed at what happens!

Form a healing circle with some of your friends. The person who is to receive the healing should sit in the centre of the circle. The other members of the group should place their quartz crystals on the floor in front of them.

Each member of the circle, at the same time, should send their love and healing thoughts to their quartz crystals and direct their crystals to pass on their healing energies to the person sitting in the middle of the circle.

If your healing circle continues to experiment with this idea you will soon find that each member of the circle will begin to receive an increasing amount of healing energy. They will feel better within themselves, with greatly improved vitality, as a result.

* The following crystal healing technique I find useful for treating emotional and sexual blockages.

Lie on the floor on your back.
Place one small quartz crystal on your throat.
Hold a quartz crystal in each hand.
Place a quartz crystal on your solar plexus.
Place one quartz crystal on each thigh, where it meets the trunk.
Place one quartz crystal on your heart chakra.

Breathe through your mouth, in a steady rhythmic manner. As you inhale, slowly 'pull' energy from your heart into your throat. Then, gently, as you exhale, 'push' energy into the base chakra from your throat. Do this seven times. If this technique causes any emotional response, allow it to happen: another block will have been removed.

* Drinking crystal water increases and balances your energy field.

You can make your own pure crystal water by placing a crystal in a glass container, adding distilled water or spring water, and placing it in the sun for a minimum of six hours. Try using a gallon jar, the type which some restaurants use for mayonnaise or pickles. A glass of crystal water, drunk with every meal, should be sufficient. More than that could cause over-stimulation.

You should take a glass of crystal water to help

For treating emotional and sexual blockages

integrate your energies before and after massage, osteopathic session or any other healing treatment.

Heating or cooling the crystal water affects the energy level, so keep it at room temperature and use your discretion when taking it with other forms of medication.

* Plants respond very quickly to the flow of crystal energy! If you have a sick or ailing plant, try the following experiment. Hold your personal quartz crystal and mentally programme the energies of the crystal to energise the plant. Then pass the single-terminated end of the crystal in a clock-wise direction around the perimeter of the plant to strengthen its biomagnetic field. Do this several times.

Now direct the energies of your crystal towards the roots of the plant and visualise a blue-white ray of light pulsating towards the plant. When you have finished – and you will know instinctively when to stop – direct the crystal energies around the plant in a clock-wise direction once more. This treatment should be repeated at least once a day and the results carefully monitored.

* On one occasion I was staying with a family the night before a crystal healing workshop. During the evening I was demonstrating my crystal wand techniques on my hostess. In the corner, behind the chair where she was sitting, was a cheese plant. When I arrived home after the workshop I received a telephone call from my excited hostess telling me that the cheese plant had grown a further six inches during the night! She even sent me photographs to prove it. The cheese plant was now reaching up and touching the ceiling and it was quite obvious from the bend in the plant's stem that a considerable amount of growth had taken place since my visit!

CHAPTER 17

An Atlantean Meditation

(This Atlantean meditation was experienced by one of my crystal healing students)

I do not yet have a name. I find myself sitting cross-legged and naked except for a crescent-shaped collar of clear crystal quartz hanging from a gold rope tied at the nape of my neck. The collar covers the upper part of my chest to my throat, and is pleasantly cool against my skin. I am alone.

The great hall that I find myself in is very long and rectangular, the decoration is utterly simple yet majestic and there are tall columns set into the wall like great pylons. There is a soft blue light, not unlike moonlight, pervading the darkness, although the hall itself is windowless and unlit. However, almost all the floor is open to the sea below and the walls of the hall dance with the reflections from the gently rippling surface. This is the source of the light. I am filled with a deep sense of peace and oneness with mother ocean. The moonlight carries me beneath the waves, sings to me of Luna, and we three – woman, ocean and moon – are eternally entwined.

As I meditate upon this, a dark fin breaks the surface at the furthest end of the pool and cuts a lightning swathe towards me. In seconds a young dolphin beaches himself half out of the water at my feet, nodding and beckoning. I take his glistening head between my hands and we commune silently together for a few moments. I am aware of his great intelligence and absolute trust and understanding. Something very special passes between us. He turns and dives into the water again and I am at his side. We swim quickly and effortlessly through the crystal clear waters, tiny silver air bubbles streaming behind us as we speed along. Although we do not touch, it is as though we are linked by an invisible film so that we move together in complete unison. We break the surface briefly for air and then plunge through the rainbow-hued shoals of fish towards the white sand of the ocean floor.

I am at home in his world: I feel as he feels, see as he sees. I rejoice in life and in the Creator. I am aware of the silky touch of the water against my skin, the almost imperceptible pull of the tides; the sudden changes in temperature where currents meet. There is not a creature living in this inner universe that is my enemy. I hear the song of other dolphins; the ancient sagas and gentle lullabies that they sing to their young.

I hear the booming resonance of faraway whales hailing us in brotherhood and greeting. The ocean is lit with phosphorescence which sparkles and darts around us in a million tiny points of light.

We swim thus for too short a time, it seems to me, until my brother turns again for home. We surface into the dim light of the hall, and before I walk from the water I embrace him with loving gratitude and give him a blessing as he leaves. I stand and watch until he is gone from sight and then, walking along the water's edge, I make my way down the hall.

As I approach the far wall two huge double doors swing open before me, and I am caught in a blaze of light streaming forth from the chamber beyond. As I walk forward, I see that I am entering a room that is almost without dimension. Here, giant crystals stand, forest-like, pulsating with purest light.

I feel a surge of power coursing through me and for a second it takes my breath away. The collar about my neck is resonating with the crystals and I find myself drawn to a great crystal slab in a clearing amongst this powerhouse.

I lie upon it and find that its surface has been carved in the very mould of my body. As I lie there, awestruck and suffused with love, wisdom and power, I see that within each giant crystal a being of light has appeared.

Their brilliance is such that I can barely distinguish their form. I am not afraid. I feel their reassurance and their encouragement reaching out to me but I am overcome with the doubt that I should be here at all – naked and ashamed in this holy place. I feel like a trespasser or interloper.

One of the beings of light communicates with me: 'Do not doubt, seeker. Do not be afraid. It is almost time.'

Another asks me: 'What is it that you seek?'

I find myself answering: 'The light beyond the light.'

He nods slowly, and then asks: 'Why do you seek this?'

'So that I may bring it unto the Earth to heal, to illumine and to nurture all life.'

Again he nods, and slowly motions for me to rise. I see before me a huge crystal, the only one without a shining brother standing within.

The being of light waves me towards it and as I reach out my hands to touch its perfect surface, I am drawn inside, into the very heart of it.

For the first time I begin to see the others clearly, and it seems to me that they are all familiar faces. But my mind is becoming so suffused with crystalline energy and the enormous power generated, that I cannot really be certain of anything any more.

From a long way away, so it seems, I hear them say that from now on, although they will be watching over me with love and tenderness, the journey to the light beyond the light is one that I must make alone.

This is where the meditation ended, at least this first part, but I feel it will be ongoing throughout my journey towards the ultimate goal.

CHAPTER 18

Moldavite

The richly coloured translucent green stone known as moldavite is the only known gemstone of extraterrestrial origin. The only recorded fall of moldavite occurred about 15 million years ago. Moldavites are the rarest of gems, perhaps even rarer than diamonds, rubies or emeralds. Since they do not originate from Earth, further discovery of new deposits seems highly unlikely.

Many people find it easy to connect with the energies of moldavite. Typically, though not always, people first experience heat radiating from the stone and a sense of pulling energy, with very strong and firm pulsations. Sometimes, when the connection is very strong, holding the stone will bring a flush to the face and neck, accompanied by the activation of the heart chakra and sometimes the higher chakras, especially the third eye.

Moldavite assists the expansion of your crystal and cosmic consciousness.

Moldavite is always made available to those who would serve it in truth. Moldavite, however, is not for everyone. Those of you reading these words who are immediately drawn to the idea of working with this fascinating stone, will intuitively realise whether or not it is right for you to acquire one!

We always have a few natural moldavite stones available for anyone wishing to acquire them; so please write to us at Crystal 2000 for further details.

CHAPTER 19

Crystal Headbands

The crystal headband helps the wearer to develop their intuitive faculty and to become telepathic and psychic.

Initially the wearer often feels completely disoriented as the headband is capable of picking up thought impressions from everyone around them. As one becomes more adept in using the crystal headband these impressions may be controlled when necessary. Distance ceases to become a barrier and impressions and ideas may be picked up, not only from people on Earth but also by extraterrestrial beings.

The crystal headband is relatively simple to construct having no moving parts. It consists of a copper band with a silver disc and a clear-tipped quartz crystal on top of the silver disc.

The tools needed to make a headband are:

A pair of pliers.
A pair of tin snips.
A tube of instant-bonding glue.

A small file.

A small drill.

The materials needed are:

A sheet of thin copper (to be cut and bent to form the band).

A one ounce silver disc or coin (obtainable from a coin shop).

A quartz crystal about one and a half inches long and about one inch in diameter.

Two narrow strips of leather, about one foot long and ¼" wide.

To make your headband begin by cutting the copper sheet to form a band. Leave enough extra copper on the front to bend and form around the crystal. Carefully file down any sharp edges as you shape and fit the band. You may want to pinch the base of the quartz crystal with the pliers to break off any rough or pointed edges. Be careful not to crack the crystal itself.

When the quartz crystal is ready, start bending the copper piece on the front of the band to fit and hold the crystal. If your crystal has one side that is flatter than the others, place the flat side against the copper. Bend the copper around the crystal for the tightest possible fit. You may have to remove the crystal and bend the copper with your pliers several times to make a good fit. You will find that it will still be slightly loose.

The next step is to slide the silver disc in behind the crystal. It should fit tightly between the crystal and copper band. If it does not then refit the crystal. If the disc is a good fit put a few drops of glue around the crystal, the silver disc and the copper band. This should seal the band tightly together for a permanent fit.

Next, at the rounded ends of the band (which should have been filed smooth earlier), drill a small hole at each end for the leather strips to fit through. Tie a knot at one end of each leather strip; a bead or two can be added to make sure that the strips cannot pull through the holes in the band. These two thongs are for tying the headband onto the head and adjusting it to fit.

You can now try out your Atlantean crystal headband.

Find a quiet, peaceful place and when you are completely relaxed place the headband on your head, adjusting the fit as you centre the silver disc/crystal upon your forehead, with the single-terminated end of the crystal pointing upwards.

After a few moments you may experience a strange feeling of disorientation. Strange sounds and impressions may flood into your mind confusingly. However, after considerable practice and perseverance, you will learn to identify specific thoughts and ideas coming to you through the ether.

A new and wondrous world awaits you!

CHAPTER 20

The Four Directions Energy Layout

This layout is used for meditations and for 'charging' objects.

You need four large quartz crystals. First, locate the true directions of north, south, east and west, using a compass if necessary.

Place one crystal representing north, one representing south, one east and one west. The single-terminated ends of each crystal should be pointing towards the centre. Sit in the centre of the four quartz crystals. Relax and feel all the stress and tension drain out of your body.

Sit in this crystal energy layout for between 15 and 20 minutes. If you feel it appropriate you might like to hold a crystal cluster in your hands. Sit in the direction you feel compelled to face; many people like to sit facing the east.

If you decide to lie down in this energy pattern, you should have your head facing north and your feet facing south. This aligns with the polarities of the earth.

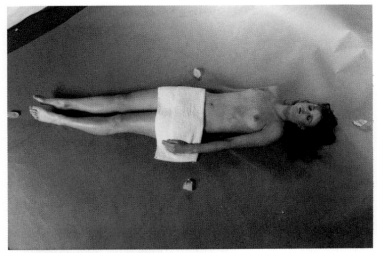

Four Directions Energy Layout

You can 'charge' crystals, water or other objects within this energy pattern and if you place objects to be charged inside a pyramid which is itself inside the four directions layout the process will be greatly amplified.

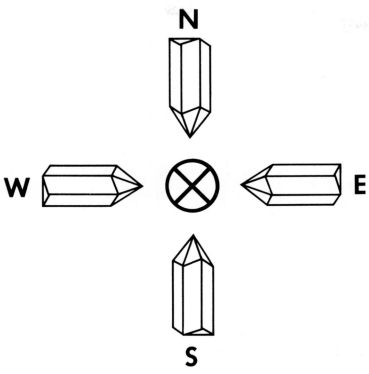

Figure 10. The Four Directions Energy Layout.

CHAPTER 21

Crystal Reflexology

First select a quartz crystal which has a good smooth single-terminated point. Then ask your patient to remove their socks or tights.

Crystal reflexology treatments may be carried out with the patient either lying on a massage couch or sitting in a comfortable chair. When using the latter method you will need to sit on a stool so that you can place your patient's feet on your lap.

Reflexology is basically a foot massage. The principle of reflexology is that the feet consist of numerous reflex points, all of which relate to specific parts of the body. A conventionally qualified reflexologist will use his hands to press into each one of these reflex points in turn. When a health problem is diagnosed the patient will often feel a sharp pain and the therapist will detect a small pea-like lump just under the surface of the skin.

In crystal reflexology, however, we do not need to be quite as precise. First we must programme our healing quartz crystal to re-balance any imbalances which might be

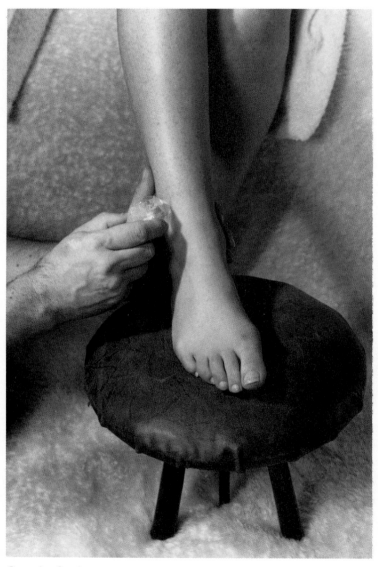

Crystal reflexology

discovered in the patient's body as the treatment proceeds.

Using the single-terminated end of the crystal the healer very gently, and without pressing too deep into the skin, starts to rotate the crystal in a clockwise direction just lightly pushing into the skin.

Starting with the sole of the left foot, the crystal is moved slowly around to the sides, lightly touching the skin all the time, and then to the upper part of the foot. All movements should be slow and deliberate. Make sure that you cover the whole surface of the foot. Repeat this procedure on the right foot.

Whenever the healer obtains a reaction from the patient he will spend a few moments directing crystalline healing energy into the appropriate reflex point.

As the crystal reflexology treatment ends the therapist takes the quartz crystal and lightly runs it over the entire surface of the foot, on the soles and on the upper part of both feet.

I suggest you spend around 30 minutes on each foot but this will depend entirely upon what you find and upon the needs of your patient.

CHAPTER 22

The White Cross Technique

If you have a boss who makes life difficult for you or if you have constant problems with a colleague, try the white cross technique.

Hold your personal quartz crystal and visualise a white cross over the head of the person you wish to influence. Then start sending out loving thoughts to the higher self of that person. Mentally affirm, 'You do not wish to harm me. You are becoming more loving; you are a much more loving person.'

As you think these words and begin to visualise a white cross in your mind's eye, you will start to notice a different expression on the person's face. If he has been very nasty towards you, he will become suddenly quiet; if he has been angry, he will start to speak more softly.

The white cross protects you; when it is present no one can harm you. Something inside the other person yearns to be soft, kind and loving in the presence of the white cross. Because of this, whenever you concentrate on

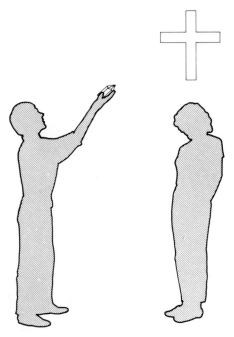

Figure 11. Mentally affirm, 'You do not wish to harm me. You are becoming more loving; you are a much more loving person.'

the divine presence within those people who wish to harm you, their expressions will be completely altered.

You can use this technique whenever you are in the company of people who are talking negatively about situations or other people. All you have to do is mentally place the white cross over their heads and they will begin to change within their own consciousness. This technique is particularly helpful when you have no wish to be part of such a discussion but feel unable to leave.

Finally, if you hold your crystal while visualising the white cross above someone's head you will find it even easier to transform their negative traits into positive ones.

CHAPTER 23

An A–Z of Crystal Information

Acupuncture

Acupuncture is an ancient form of Chinese healing in which needles are inserted into certain points on the body (usually called meridian points) to affect the energy flow throughout the body. The change in energy can bring healing or relaxation to specific organs depending on where the needles are inserted.

Acupuncturists can now be found throughout the world.

Acupressure is a more recent form of this therapy in which pressure is used rather than needles.

Some crystal healers lightly place the single-terminated end of their quartz crystal on these meridian points and project healing energy through these points into the patient's body – with excellent results.

Alchemy

Alchemy is the science of transformation and transmutation, involving, in particular, the infusion of greater degrees of light into matter and consciousness.

Allopathic medicine

This form of medicine, most commonly practised in the western world, treats disease according to its symptoms, usually with medication or surgery.

Alternative healing

This is any method of healing that treats the whole person and tries to establish the root causes of disease, rather than just the symptoms. Hence the phrase, Holistic Natural Health Practitioner; holistic coming from holos, the Greek word for whole. This term includes all natural health therapies from crystal healing and massage to osteopathy and homoeopathy.

Amulet

Amulets are quartz crystals programmed for protection and personal power. People who are moving strongly on their spiritual path are drawn to using amulets.

The crystal Mandala Power Amulet creates a powerful protective force field around one which can be dowsed at over 100 feet. It neutralises negative thought-forms from others. It enables you to be in places, such as hospitals, where strong negative emotions have been embedded. It stimulates the immune system and reduces emotional stress. It increases spiritual and psychic powers and attunes you to the natural forces of the universe. Amulets also serve as a powerful protection against the emotional attacks from people around you.

Anisotrophy
Having properties that are different in different directions, e.g. the strength of wood along the grain differs from that across the grain.

Ankh
A cross which has a loop for its upper vertical arm. Ankhs were used in ancient Egypt as hand mirrors and were a symbol of knowledge of, and the ability to control, energies.

Apas
Water principle.

Astral travelling
Travel undertaken by one's etheric body, usually during sleep, to realms outside physical reality.

Astrology
An ancient system of divination and life knowledge based on the positions of the planets. Each individual's original astrological make-up is determined by the time of birth, but this changes with the passage of time and the movement of the planets through the solar system.

Astrophysics
A branch of astronomy concerned with the chemical and physical constitution of celestial bodies.

Atlantis

Atlantis was an ancient continent that, it is thought, existed in the Atlantic ocean. It is believed to have been situated from the east coast of America to where Greece is today.

Although Atlantis is considered by scientists to be purely legendary, there are many indications that Atlantis really did exist and was once a thriving continent, whose technology was greatly superior to that of the 20th century.

Aura

A combination of the etheric and spiritual bodies results in what is known as the human aura. One dictionary defines the aura as 'an air, a subtle influence or quality emanating from or surrounding a person or object'.

Kirlian photography is said to demonstrate this electromagnetic field which surrounds humans, plants, animals and other matter with a coronal image. It is believed that the human soul is contained within the aura and it is both an ancient and universal belief that the aura survives man beyond physical death.

The soul radiates the colour vibrations of the three bodies. For those with clairvoyant vision, the clarity of the colours emitted indicates the health and well-being of both the spiritual and physical bodies. Besides determining health, it is believed that information may also be obtained with regard to a person's past incarnations, future events and spiritual guides.

Automatic writing

Automatic writing is writing done by a 'sensitive', or medium, who is given information to communicate by a spirit guide. In some instances the 'sensitive' is completely unaware of what he or she is writing.

Ayurvedic medicine

An ancient form of alternative healing originating in India. In Sanskrit the word ayurveda means 'the science of life'.

Balancing

Bringing the dualistic or discordant aspects of an energy field into harmony with each other, thus producing an equilibrium that encourages and enhances health and strength.

Bio-energy

Bio-energy is a pulsating energy that permeates and penetrates all living beings. This same force is also called 'chi', 'prana', 'sacred energy' and 'orgone energy'.

Biomolecular

Chemical activity in the subatomic cellular structure.

Blue quartz

A rare form of quartz mostly found in Brazil.

Blue quartz was used in Lemuria to open the heart chakra and to increase longevity. It is associated with karmic patterns concerning affairs of the heart. General healing and the removal of toxins from the body are amplified with the use of blue quartz.

Blue quartz aligns the heart and throat chakras and all subtle bodies. Those who suffer from depression or an unnatural fear of growing old often receive great benefit from treatment involving blue quartz. Blue quartz opens one to a true expression of one's spiritual qualities, with self-expression abilities and creativity increasing.

Cabochon
A bead or gem cut in convex form and highly polished, but not faceted.

Centring
The process of balancing a person's energy field through the use of various methods like smudging, breathing and meditation. Often used synonymously with balancing.

Channelling
Channelling is done by a 'sensitive' who receives information and ideas from beings not of this world. They are often called 'interdimensional beings', 'spirit forces' or 'entities'.

Chi
A Chinese word meaning 'life energy'.

Clairsentience
The power of faculty to sense people's physical and psychic states.

Clairvoyance
The ability to perceive things beyond the range of the ordinary senses. The word literally means 'clear seeing'. Clairvoyants use their gifts and abilities to communicate with discarnate beings and to convey messages from these spirits to the people for whom they are intended.

Corundum

A very hard aluminium oxide mineral. It is used especially as an abrasive but in its coloured form of, for example, ruby and sapphire it is also used as a gemstone.

Coven

A group of people who believe in reincarnation, the Mother God, natural magic and the control of the elements to better themselves.

Crystal balls

A crystal ball is a sphere shaped out of natural quartz crystal. It may also refer to the glass ball that is commonly used by fortune-tellers or gypsies to see into the future.

Crystal clusters

A crystal cluster is a formation of many single-terminated quartz crystals that share a common base. The energy that emanates from this formation is amplified because multiple crystals are involved.

Crystal clusters generate wonderful energy if placed in a room. They help to raise the vibrations and 'lighten' the atmosphere. Other crystals and gemstones may be cleansed and re-charged by placing them on a crystal cluster.

Crystal dreaming

Herkimer diamonds and amethyst clusters are great for dreamwork. Keep a pad and pen by your bed each night, so that in the morning you will be able to recall your dreams and write them down before you forget them! With continual practice you will become increasingly proficient in recalling your nightly dreams the moment you open your eyes in the morning. Try and keep a cassette recorder handy. Dream memories fade very quickly but with a little bit of forethought you can capture your dream experiences for ever.

Many messages come to us in our dreams. Any quartz crystal will enhance the quality of your dreams and both herkimer diamonds and amethyst clusters are excellent for that purpose. It helps if you first programme your stone for 'dream recall'. Every night thereafter you must continue to tell yourself that you will remember your dreams.

You can make or buy a bag in which to hold your stone at night while you are asleep. The bag can be a small one for wearing around your neck, or a larger one that fits inside your pillow case. Either way, as long as your stone is within your energy field it will continue to affect you.

Crystal hypnosis

Certain quartz crystals may be 'programmed' so that when the single-terminated end of the crystal is directed towards the patient's third eye chakra they will find it very difficult to keep their eyes open and will gradually fall into a deep and peaceful trance. Under crystal hypnosis many past-life regression experiences occur.

Crystallography

The science of crystal form and structure.

Crystal skulls

These are skulls carved from large piece of quartz crystal. They are said to originate from various ancient cultures, predominantly South American or Atlantean. They are considered to contain great energy and power. The most famous crystal skull, generally believed to be the oldest, is the Mitchell-Hedges Skull from Canada. There is also a crystal skull to be found in the Museum of Mankind, Burlington Gardens, London.

Crystal tuning
A technique used to create harmonic resonance between human beings and crystals.

Crystal water
Water in which gem stones have been left to stand, in sunlight, for several hours. The water thus obtained will contain energy from the gemstones.

Deva
A nature spirit associated with beings in nature that exist on the physical plane.

Divination
A way of gaining insight into the future using supernatural means.

Dodecahedral
A 12-sided figure with diamond-shaped faces.

Double-terminated quartz crystals
Double-terminated quartz crystals are crystals with a termination point at both ends. Such crystals complete a circuit of energy. Energy enters and exits at both ends. They are very powerful when used in crystal configurations.

Dream crystal
A quartz crystal used in dreaming or to bring about altered states of awareness.

Drusy
Covered with a layer of crystals, usually quartz.

Earthkeeper crystals
Earthkeeper crystals are very large and heavy quartz crystals which contain infinite knowledge, understanding and energy. They are very special crystals only a few having been discovered this century.

Electromagnetism
The study of the magnetic forces produced by electricity.

Elementals
The elementals are the four elements – earth, air, fire and water – and the things composed of these elements such as stones, crystals and magma.

   The elemental kingdom is believed to be the first kingdom on the earth; the building blocks from which all other life stems. It is considered the most independent of the four kingdoms because it can exist alone.

Elements
An element is a substance composed of atoms having an identical number of protons in each nucleus. There are currently more than 100 elements recognised by science.

Energies

Energies are the formless, subatomic, primordial essences that permeate all of creation. From this original energy comes all of the secondary ones such as gravity, electricity and magnetism. This energy eventually creates as well as fills all subsequent forms.

Energy balancing

A process of harmonising the various subtle and gross energies within a system, individual or structure to produce optimum health on all levels of being.

Entity

A defined being, whether corporeal or disembodied.

Etheric body

Our skin is surrounded by a cocoon of energy radiating approximately four inches away from our physical body.

Clairvoyants or sensitives can 'see' this body as a violet-grey mist. This casing, or webbing, as it is sometimes called, contains the energies of our physical body. It has the capacity to draw in and hold the vital energies from the sun and earth which are in turn fed into our physical structures.

The condition of the physical body can be determined by examining this webbing. When a person is in perfect physical and spiritual health there are no breaks or imperfections in the etheric surface. However, should any disharmony of either a physical or spiritual nature occur, tears or holes will appear. If these defects go undetected, disease or pain can become apparent in the physical body.

Ethers
A subtle, all-pervading, massless medium close to, but not defined by, the physical plane.

Fire crystals
Used by ancient priests and scientists to divide, augment or multiply energies for therapeutic treatments of body and mind. Fire crystals also affect the earth's etheric grid or ley line system.

Flower essence healing
A system of healing using floral essences, in homoeopathic proportions, that act on the root causes of the disease. The system was established by Dr Edward Bach who believed that all diseases stemmed from disturbances in a person's emotional or etheric body.

Gem
A jewel, precious or semi-precious stone cut and polished for ornamentation.

Gemology
The science of gems.

Generator quartz crystals
These are large single-terminated quartz crystal points. They usually average about six inches in length, four inches in diameter and weigh about two pounds although they can be considerably larger. These crystals are wonderful for using in group meditations.

Giza
Place in Egypt; home of three major pyramids as well as the Sphinx.

Glass
A non-crystalline, amorphous substance of sand, soda and lime, often transparent, and created by fusion under intense heat.

Grounding
A process by which a person or object is reconnected with the energy of the earth and the physical plane.

Hand scanning
The use of one's hands to determine the shape and quality of an energy field radiating from a person or object.

Hatha Yoga
An ancient system of physical and breathing exercises originating in India.

Hertz Scale
A scale to measure units of frequency equal to one cycle per second.

Holistic healing
Any method of healing that treats the whole person and the root cause of the disease. The term is used synonymously with alternative healing.

Homoeopathy

A system of natural health and healing in which minute amounts of natural substances are used to treat a person by activating their body's natural defences against disease.

Inclusions

Quartz crystals, like most minerals, grow beneath the surface of the earth in beds of igneous rock. The crystals will often contain impurities from minerals such as copper, tourmaline, beryl and other semi-precious stones due to sharing the growing space. These 'inclusions' lead to an altering of the vibrational energy of the stone when used for work involving the higher consciousness.

Interdimensional beings

Disembodied beings who exist on other planes but teach on earth by using humans as their channel.

Kabbalah

A system of Jewish theosophy, mysticism and thaumaturgy that is both medieval and modern. It is marked by a belief in creation through emanation and a cipher method of interpreting scripture.

Kinesiology

The study of the mechanics of body movement. It often refers to a method of diagnosis in which the effect of substances or treatments on a patient is measured by their relative muscle strength when exposed to that substance or treatment.

Kingdoms

These refer to various sections of the circle of life. The usual reference by indigenous people is to the four kingdoms, which consists of the elementals, plants, animals and humans.

Kirlian photography

This process was pioneered by Nikola Tesla and developed by Semyon Kirlian, a Czechoslovakian. It is a method of photography using a high-voltage, low amperage field of 50,000 volts or more by which the life force or bio-energy field can be made visible. This method can be used to show any increase in the energy field of a subject after crystal healing techniques have been used. Any object can be photographed and the resultant changes observed.

One of the leading researchers on the subject of Kirlian photography is Harry Oldfield from London, who is also the Principal of the School of Electro-Crystal Therapy.

Kundalini

Kundalini is a yoga term for a very powerful concentration of life energy which is said to coil in the root chakra, like a serpent of fire. As we achieve spiritual awareness, this force moves up our spine, opening and enlivening each chakra in turn.

Lapidary

A cutter, polisher, or engraver of precious stones.

Laser

Light amplification by stimulated emission of radiation. A device that generates and projects highly coherent, ordered frequencies of light.

Lead crystal

Lead crystal is created by mixing together molten sand and lead. The molecular alignment of this mixture is random and does not have any of the therapeutic healing properties of quartz crystals.

Ley lines

Invisible lines of magnetic power around Earth, believed to be associated with prehistoric mounds, equivalent to the acupuncture meridian system of the human body.

Life energy

The vital force of all living things.

Liquid crystal

A liquid solution that converts to crystal when a slight change of energy is applied. A common use of liquid crystal is in computer displays and watches.

Machu Picchu

An ancient and legendary isolated temple situated in the high Andes of Peru.

Magic

The use of ceremony and ritual to affect energy is the major function of magic. Crystals interact with energy and can,

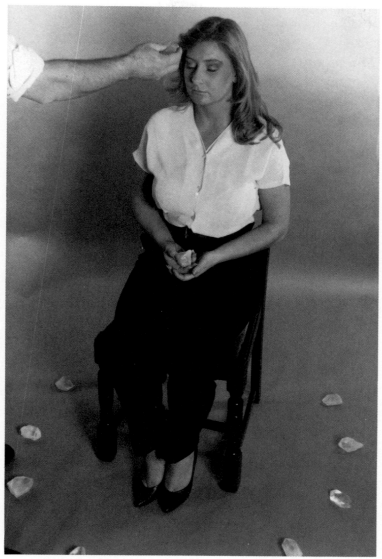

Crystal Hypnosis (see page 204)

therefore, he used in magical ceremonies. Magic is an emotive word with many undeserved attachments.

Magician
A person skilled in or practising magic.

Magma
The molten matter beneath the earth's crust which, when cooled, becomes igneous rock.

Magnetism
Magnetism is a force that either pulls living things together or pushes them apart. It derives its power from the electrical property of all atoms. There are three types of magnetism affecting minerals:

   1) Diamagnetic: tending to become magnetized in a direction at right angles to the applied magnetic field.
   2) Ferromagnetic: minerals or rocks having a strong ability to attract other minerals (iron is ferromagnetic; north pole magnetism attracts south pole magnetism).
   3) Paramagnetic: tending to become weakly magnetized so as to lie parallel to a magnetic field force.

Mantra
A repetitive sound or chant usually used to aid in a meditation process.

Massage crystals
These are single-terminated crystals that have been polished. The flat base has been rounded off so that it can be held in the hand more comfortably. The single-

terminated end still contains the six facets but, in most cases, the point has been smoothed down.

Massage crystals are often used in crystal massage, shiatsu, acupressure, polarity therapy and reflexology. The crystal point is held over an imbalanced area and gentle pressure is then applied. Some healers are able to perform 'psychic surgery' with their massage crystals.

Massive
An irregular form without distinct characteristics and not visibly crystalline.

Matrix
The natural material in which a crystal, gem, metal, or fossil, originates, is developed, or contained.

Medicine
A European word for a wide variety of indigenous systems of philosophy, healing, religion, working with the elements, divination, psychology and magic.

Medicine man or woman
The spiritual leader of a tribe or clan who fulfils the functions performed today by doctors, clergy, psychologists, magicians, clairvoyants, visionaries and ceremonialists.

Medicine wheel
A medicine wheel is a circle, usually of stones, that was the ceremonial centre for many indigenous peoples. Used in a spiritual context the medicine wheel encompasses the circle of life and all the sacred energy that flows through it.

Medium

A medium is someone who can communicate with those in the spirit world. These spirit beings – or guides – may be relatives or friends of the person seeking to communicate. They may also be higher evolved souls who wish to impart wisdom, understanding and esoteric knowledge. Mediums may either be conscious while transmitting spirit messages or in a semi-conscious state called trance.

Meridian

A subtle line along which energy flows. It can be likened to a wire or conduit, circulating the life force into and around the physical body.

Metallurgy

The science concerned with the production, purification and properties of metals and their application.

Metaphysics

The theoretical philosophy of being and knowing.

Mineralogy

The scientific study of minerals: their classifications, distinguishing characteristics, crystallography and properties both chemical and physical.

Minerals

Naturally occurring, inorganic, homogeneous substances that have a specific chemical composition as well as a characteristic crystalline structure, colour and hardness. There are over 3,000 on Earth.

Mohs' scale

A scale for measuring the hardness of minerals. Soft minerals, like talc, have a rating of one, while hard minerals, like diamonds, have a rating of 10.

Nadi

Subtle nerve centres.

Native

A philosophy originating from the traditional ways of the tribal, earth-oriented people of the world, from whichever continent. Native may also refer to a person who can trace his ancestry to such tribal peoples.

Needle crystal

A long, narrow, perfectly formed, clear, single-terminated crystal which can be used to forcefully move energy or to remove blockages from the body. A needle crystal will be approximately four times as long as it is wide.

Orgone

The primordial, mass-free, preatomic energy that was first discovered and scientifically demonstrated by Dr Wilhelm Reich.

Path

A metaphor for the direction of a seeker's life.

Pendants

Hanging crystal attached to a necklace. When worn over the heart chakra, which extends from the hollow of the throat to the juncture of the breastbone, it will stimulate the thymus gland and thus the immune system. The pendant chain should be made from conductive metal, such as gold or silver, or other natural material like silk, leather, cotton or wool. A crystal worn over the heart chakra will display an increase in energy fields of from three to five times the normal level when measured by both Kirlian photography and dowsing.

Phantom crystals
A phantom crystal is a crystal within which another fully formed crystal has grown.

Piezoelectricity
The characteristic, possessed by certain crystals or other substances of emitting an electrical charge when stressed. When under stress in one plane the material will discharge electricity in a plane perpendicular to the plane of stress. This characteristic demonstrates that the forces holding the crystal lattice together are electric as well as molecular and ionic.

Placebo
An ineffective medication prescribed for psychological relief rather than treatment of the physical disorder. Also used in controlled experiments.

Polarity
The quality inherent in the human body which exhibits opposite or contrasting properties or powers in opposite or contrasting directions or parts.

Polished quartz

Crystal healers are unable to agree whether or not polished quartz (i.e. cut and faceted by machine) contains more energy and power than natural quartz crystal. Natural quartz crystals do possess the obvious advantage that their vibrations are undisturbed by human handling. Many crystal healers believe that the quartz crystal in its most natural form is the only way in which it should ever be used. Natural quartz crystals are also less expensive to purchase, can be mined personally, and are far more accessible than polished quartz crystals.

Polished quartz crystals do, however, have some benefits. They are aesthetically pleasing as all their facets and points are intact and unchipped. The milkiness found in natural quartz is missing, the base is smooth and they can be shaped into forms with more than six facets.

The late Marcel Vogel, the famous crystal healer who was Chief Scientist for IBM, discovered that by cutting and faceting, the crystal's storage capacity was increased. This made it a more directed crystal tool for performing extensive etheric healings and mind thought projections.

Prana

The Sanskrit/Hindu word meaning 'life energy'.

Psychometry

A method of receiving impressions about a person or place by holding something that comes from that person or location.

Pyramid facet crystals

These are usually clear quartz crystals which are used for meditation and dream work. A facet may have one or more triangle formations on the surface. There is a tremendous amount of information stored within these quartz crystals.

Pyramidology

The science of pyramidical energy dynamics.

Radionics

An early name given to psionics when applied to the electronic-type black box machines invented in the 1940s and 1950s.

Rainbow crystal

A crystal with inclusions that cause one or more spectrums to be seen within the crystal when held under a certain light.

Rosicrucian

Philosophical order in the 15th century devoted to esoteric wisdom with an emphasis on spiritual enlightenment.

Sacred energy

The vital force that is within and around everything.

Scrying

An ancient method of divining using crystals, a crystal ball, water, fire or coals.

Sex and crystals

After the instinct to survive the sex drive is the strongest drive we possess. Our sex drive is an integral and important part of our emotional, physical and mental energies. A satisfactory and healthy sex life requires a balanced, harmonised mind, body and spirit.

Your quartz crystal can assist you at all levels. If you are able to balance all your energy centres correctly then sex will fall into its rightful place as a natural function of being human. If your sex drive is weak, your quartz crystal will strengthen it. If it is too strong, then your quartz crystal will help you to achieve a proper balance.

Rose quartz is the gemstone found most effective for emotional balance in heart problems. Citrine quartz is used very successfully in balancing the lower energy centres, including the sexual chakra. Wearing either or both rose quartz and citrine pendants will help you to maintain perfect emotional balance.

Shamans

A Russian word now commonly used to denote a medicine man or woman or a person of extraordinary power.

Single-terminated quartz

Natural quartz crystals come in many sizes, colours and shapes but all have six sides and two ends. The flat end is the base of the crystal that was rooted into the earth. The other end comes to a six-faceted point. This is the terminated end of the crystal. Energy is focused and emanates from the terminated end. Single-terminated quartz crystals are used by many people for meditation and healing practices.

Smudging

A method of cleansing, centring and balancing an energy field through the use of smoke from burning herbs, usually sage, cedar and sweet grass.

Spirit forces

Refers to beings and powers who dwell outside the physical level of existence. These may be people who have died, nature spirits that have always existed or the elemental powers.

Solar system

The sun and the celestial bodies, including Earth, whose motion it governs.

Solar plexus

A nerve centre in the abdomen situated in the pit of the stomach, also called the instinctual mind, gut or abdominal brain.

Spiritual bodies

Around the etheric body, often extending for several feet, flow the energies of the emotional and mental bodies. These two vibrational fields are called the spiritual bodies.

The emotional body (also called the astral body) stores such feelings as fear, courage, joy, sorrow, love and hate.

Liberating emotions are released to the physical structure by individual triggers. For example, the death of a close friend may elicit the response of sorrow. The more intense this feeling, the more messages will be relayed from the emotional body to its physical counterpart. A corresponding physical response may thus be crying, shaking or sickness.

The mental body can be described as 'the essence of active intelligence. It has qualities such as rules, regulations, evaluation, discipline, control and judgement'. Like the emotional body, any disharmony can result in physical symptoms. For example, if a person commits an immoral act (an act that conflicts with his or her beliefs) then that person may unconsciously punish the physical self with disease.

The mental body acts as a balance between the etheric and emotional aspects by utilising 'active intelligence, discipline, memory, judgement and discrimination to evaluate and process data'. It decides what will and will not filter into the other bodies.

A chain reaction can occur when the emotional and mental parts of the spiritual bodies direct the etheric which in turn affects the condition of the physical structure. In order for us to be in perfect holistic health, a balance between all bodies needs to be achieved and then maintained.

Subtle body
The etheric or energy body.

Subtle fields
Certain energies or forces emitted from living beings.

Synergy
The combined effect of different agents that exceeds the sum of their individual parts.

Synthetic crystals

Crystals can be 'grown' in a laboratory from a slice of natural crystal by placing it in a tank with liquid and crushed natural crystal and then exposing it to pressure and an electrical current.

Synthetic crystals can be grown in days whereas an equivalent natural crystal will take thousands of years to grow.

The natural quartz crystal in its thousands of years of growth will have absorbed all the energy of the earth's changes. This energy gives the natural crystal abilities and information which the synthetic crystal cannot possess. The synthetic crystal is purely a clone, artificially reproduced from the real thing. It is like a baby with no grooves in the brain. It has no intelligence, no information and operates only on stimulus and response. It will function on the lower energy levels but not on the higher levels.

Synthetic crystals could be used to send energy to the second level, the electric sheath directly around the physical body but it would be unable to work on the emotional or higher mental levels. In a computer memory, the synthetics begin to lose their information storage abilities after several years. Natural crystals never lose that ability.

Tabular crystals

These are quartz crystals with four narrow sides and two broad sides. Some are found in double-terminated form. Tabular crystals are used as 'bridgers'. They connect us to a much higher realm of conscious awareness. They may also be placed between the chakras to help with chakra balancing.

Talisman

A talisman is a stone, which has some type of design inscribed on it, used to assist in some ritual or ceremony by amplifying, channelling or causing some catalytic process to take place.

Telepathy

A method of communicating thoughts or feelings using means outside the normal senses.

Tejas

Fire principle.

Termination

The point which is formed where the sides of a crystal meet. A single-terminated crystal has one point and an unpointed base. A double-terminated crystal has two points – one at each end – and no base.

Third eye

A point between the eyebrows, relating to the pineal gland in the forebrain, the seat of inspiration, superconsciousness, intuition or knowledge without physical proof.

Trigger crystal

A single-terminated crystal that has a smaller crystal on one of its faces near to the base. This smaller crystal is the trigger which, when pressed, is said to amplify the power coming from the larger crystal.

Twin crystal
Two crystals that have grown together from the same base, one growing through the other.

Vayu
Air principle.

Way
A metaphor for the direction of a seeker's life or for the manner in which a seeker approaches life or a particular task.

White crystal medicine
One of four great medicine practices of the American Indian tradition where crystals are considered to be related to the Earth's 'brain' cells.

X-crystal
Two quartz crystals that have grown together in such a way that they form an X shape. This crystal is considered to have particular abilities for bringing male and female energy into balance.

Y-crystal
Two quartz crystals that have grown together to form a Y shape. Y-crystals are said to have the same function as X-crystals.

Yoga
An ancient practice originating in the Orient that strives to bring about an integration between physical, mental, emotional and spiritual energies.

CHAPTER 24

Crystal Healing Certificated Course

Since it was first suggested to me some years ago by the Institute of Complementary Medicine in London that I should pioneer the first Crystal healing Certificated Course, a great deal of water has passed under the bridge.

Although other crystal healers have also introduced certificate courses, the Crystal 2000 Crystal Healing Certificate Course still remains one of only two courses which have been officially ratified and approved by the International Association of Crystal Healing Therapists.

The Crystal 2000 Crystal Healing Certificated Course consists of nine non-residential weekends. All students wishing to become fully qualified crystal healing therapists must complete all nine weekend courses. Once the student has attended the first weekend (The Foundation Course) he or she may complete the remainder of the weekends in any order they choose. At the conclusion of each weekend the student will be awarded one full credit. When nine full credits have been obtained the student may then apply to sit the final examinations. These consist of a three-hour written examination and a three-hour practical examination. Successful students who pass both the written and practical examinations will be awarded a Crystal Healing Certificate and may add the letters M.Crys.H after their name.

The Crystal 2000 Crystal Healing Certificated Course consists of the following nine weekends:

a) Foundation weekend
b) Crystal configurations – 1
c) Crystal configurations – 2
d) Crystal massage
e) Colour crystal healing
f) Gem elixirs
g) Regression
h) Research
i) Anatomy and physiology

If you are interested in becoming a fully qualified crystal healing therapist, prospectuses can be obtained from the following address:

Crystal 2000
37 Bromley Road
St Annes-on-Sea
Lancashire FY8 1PQ
England

CHAPTER 25

Crystal Healing Correspondence Course

The Crystal 2000 Crystal Healing Correspondence Course had been specifically designed for people who wish to learn about crystal healing but who are unable to attend the Crystal 2000 Crystal Healing Certificate Course Weekends.

Course Director
Geoffrey Keyte

No time limit
You can work at your own pace and take as long as you wish to complete the syllabus.

Certificate
You may take the examination at the conclusion of the twelfth lesson. Students achieving in excess of 60 per cent are awarded their certificate.

Course method

On registering you will receive the first two lessons, a list of recommended books and gemstones and detailed notes. As you complete and return the homework for each lesson, we send you the next one – together with our comments and advice on your previous work.

Individual tutors

Every student is assigned an individual tutor who is always happy to answer any questions which may arise during the course.

Reading material

Full notes accompany each lesson, but students will also need to purchase up to six books recommended by Crystal 2000.

Membership

All registered students will be entitled to become full members of Crystal 2000.

Syllabus

Lesson 1

Historical perspective – Atlantis – Lemuria – Crystal wands and headbands – Atlantean healing temples – Bermuda triangle – earthkeeper crystals – record keeper crystals

Lesson 2

Choosing crystals – cleansing crystals – dedicating crystals – manifesting – vibrational energies

Lesson 3
Programming crystals – the healing properties of gemstones

Lesson 4
Colour crystal healing – birthstones – crystal numerology

Lesson 5
Elestials – channelling crystals – laser wands – dowsing with crystals

Lesson 6
The chakras – electrocrystal therapy – crystal sound therapy – the thymus

Lesson 7
Aura scanning – crystal configurations

Lesson 8
Crystal grids – bed patterns – room patterns

Lesson 9
Crystal triangulations – a pattern for relationships – the healing circle – crystal hypnosis

Lesson 10
Crystal meditation – crystal dreaming – planting crystals – crystal reflexology

Lesson 11
The white cross technique – blue quartz – the four directions energy layout

Lesson 12
Moldavite – pyramids – the total healing experience

Examination
After completing the twelfth lesson, students may take a three-hour written examination in their own home. Students achieving a pass mark in excess of 60 per cent are awarded a certificate.

Optional sessions
Each year we arrange one residential weekend for correspondence course students who want to obtain 'hands-on' experience in the use of crystals and gemstones for healing purposes.

From time to time, as new information and data becomes available, we also invite students to participate in advanced crystal healing sessions.

If you would like to enrol for the correspondence course – or require further information – please write to us at:

UK address
Geoffrey Keyte, 37 Bromley Road, St Annes-on-Sea, Lancashire, FY8 1PQ, England

US address
Geoffrey Keyte, The Mystical Crystal, 217 Park Avenue, Box 332, Worcester, MA 01609-2243, USA

Email: 100347.2724@compuserve.com

World Wide Web:-
http://www.nitehawk.com/Mystical.Crystal/

Bibliography

Alper, Frank; *Exploring Atlantis (Vols 1–3)*, Arizona Metaphysical Society, Phoenix, USA, 1982–1985.

Badgley, Laurence; *Energy Medicine*, Human Energy Press, 1985.

Badgley, Laurence; *Chakra Chrome*, Human Energy Press, 1984.

Baer, Randall and Vicki; *The Windows of Light*, Harper & Row, New York, 1984.

Baer, Randall and Vicki; *The Crystal Connection*, Harper & Row, New York, 1987.

Bailey, Alice A; *Esoteric Healing*, Lucis Publishing Company.

Bailey, Alice A; *Treatise on Cosmic Fire*, Lucis Publishing Company.

Berlitz, Charles; *The Philadelphia Experiment*, Granada Publishing, 1980.

Berlitz, Charles; *The Mystery of Atlantis*, Granada Publishing, 1977.

Berlitz, Charles; *Mysteries From Forgotten Worlds*, Souvenir Press, 1972.

Berlitz, Charles; *Without A Trace*, Souvenir Press, 1977.

Bhattacharya, Benoytosh; *Gem Therapy*, Calcutta: Firma KLM Private Limited, 1981.

Bonewitz, Ra; *Cosmic Crystals*, Turnstone Press, Wellingborough, Northants, 1983.

Bonewitz, Ra; *The Cosmic Crystal Spiral*, Element Books, Shaftesbury, Dorset, 1986.

Bonewitz, Ra; *The Crystal Heart*, Aquarian Press, 1989.

Bowman, Catherine; *Crystal Awareness*, Llewellyn.

Bramwell, James; *Lost Atlantis*, Cobden-Sanderson, 1937.

Breasted, J. H.; *History of Egypt*, Hodder and Stoughton.

Brennan, Martin; *The Stars and the Stones*, Thames and Hudson, 1983.

Bridgman-Metchum, D; *Atlantis, The Book of the Angels*, Swan Sonnenschein, 1900.

Bryant, Page; *Crystals and Their Uses*, Sun Books, Santa Fe, New Mexico, USA, 1984.

Caldecott, Moyra; *Crystal Legends*, Aquarian Press.

Cannon, Dolores; *Jesus and The Essenes*, Gateway Books, 1992.

Cayce, Edgar; *Gems and Stones*, Association of Research and Enlightenment, Virginia Beach, USA, 1979.

Cayce, Edgar; *Edgar Cayce on Atlantis*, Association of Research and Enlightenment, Virginia Beach, USA, 1962.

Cayce, Edgar; *Edgar Cayce on Reincarnation*, Association of Research and Enlightenment, Virginia Beach, USA, 1971.

Cayce, Edgar; *Edgar Cayce on E.S.P.*, Aquarian Press, 1989.

Cayce, Edgar; *Edgar Cayce on Dreams*, Aquarian Press, 1989.

Cayce, Edgar; *Edgar Cayce on Remembering Past Lives*, Aquarian Press, 1990.

Cayce, Edgar; *Edgar Cayce on the Mysteries of the Mind*, Aquarian Press, 1990.

Chandu, Jack; *The Pendulum Book*, C. W. Daniel, 1988.

Chocron, Daya Sarai; *Healing The Heart*, Samuel Weiser, York Beach, Maine, USA, 1989.

Church, Connie; *Crystal Love*, Villard Books, 1988.

Churchward, James; *The Lost Continent of Mu*, C. W. Daniel, Saffron Walden, Essex 1987.

Churchward, James; *The Sacred Symbols of Mu*, C. W. Daniel, Saffron Walden, Essex 1988.

Churchward, James; *Children of Mu*, C. W. Daniels, 1988.

Churchward, James; *Cosmic Forces of Mu*, Vol. 1, C. W. Daniel, Saffron Walden, Essex 1992.

Churchward, James; *Cosmic Forces of Mu*, Vol. 2, C. W. Daniel, Saffron Walden, Essex 1992.

Clow, Barbara Hand; *The Heart of the Christos*, Bear and Co, 1989.

Cottrell, Leonard; *Life Under The Pharaohs*, Pan Books, 1955.

Crow, W. B.; *Precious Stones*, Aquarian Press, 1980.

Damigeron; *The Virtues of Stones*, Ars Obscura, 1989.

Davidson, John; *Subtle Energy*, C. W. Daniel, Saffron Walden, Essex 1986.

Davidovits, Joseph and Margie Morris; *The Pyramids: An Enigma Solved*, Hippocrene Books, 1988.

Deaver, Korra; *Rock Crystal*, Samuel Weiser, York Beach, Maine, USA, 1985.

Donnelly, Ignatius; *Atlantis, The Antediluvian World*, Dover Books, 1976.

Edwards, J. E. S.; *The Pyramids of Egypt*, Penguin.

Erman, A; *A Handbook of Egyptian Religion*, Macmillan.

Finch, Elizabeth; *The Psychic Value of Gemstones*, Esoteric Publications, 1980.

Galanopoulos, A. G. and Edward Bacon; *Atlantis: The Truth Behind the Legend*, Indianopolis: Bobbs-Merrill, 1969.

Galde, Phyllis; *Crystal Healing*, Llewellyn, 1991.

Garvin, Richard; *The Crystal Skull*, Pocket Books, New York, USA, 1974.

Gerber, Richard; *Vibrational Medicine*, Bear & Co. 1988.

Gimbel, Theo; *Healing Through Colour*, C. W. Daniel, Saffron Walden, Essex 1980.

Gimbel, Theo; *Form, Sound, Colour and Healing*, C. W. Daniel, Saffron Walden, Essex 1987.

Glick, Joel; *Healing Stoned*, Brotherhood of Life, Albuquerque, New Mexico, USA, 1981.

Gurudas; *Gem Elixirs and Vibrational Healing* (Vols. 1 and 2), Cassandra Press, Boulder, Colorado, USA, 1985 and 1986.

Haich, Elisabeth; *Initiation*, Seed Center, 1960.

Harford, Milewski; *The Crystal Sourcebook*, Mystic Crystal Publications, 1987.

Harold, Edmund; *Crystal Healing*, Aquarian Press.

Holbeche, Soozi; *Power of Gems and Crystals*, Piatkus.

Hurtak, J. J.; *The Book of Knowledge: The Keys of Enoch*, Academy of Future Sciences, 1982.

Irwin, Neil; *Understanding Crystals*, Aquarian Press.

Isaacs, Thelma; *Gemstones, Crystals and Healing*, Lorien House, 1982.

Isaacs, Thelma; *Gemstone & Crystal Energies*, Lorien House, 1989.

Jameison, Bryan; *Explore Your Past Lives*, Van Nuys, California, 1976.

Keyte, Geoffrey; *The Healing Crystal*, Cassells, London, 1989.

Kilner, W. J.; *The Aura*, Samuel Weiser, York Beach, Maine, USA, 1973.

Kunz, George; *The Curious Lore of Precious Stones*, Dover, New York, USA, 1971.

Kunz, George; *Gems & Precious Stones of North America*, Dover, New York, 1968.

Leadbeater, C. W.; *The Chakras*, Theosophical Publishing, 1927.

Lehner, Mark; *The Egyptian Heritage*, ARE Press, 1974.

Littlefield, Charles; *Man, Minerals and Masters*, Sun Books, 1987.

Lorusso, Julia & Joel Glick; *Healing Stoned*, Brotherhood of Life, 1980.

Markham, Ursula; *Fortune Telling By Crystals*, Aquarian Press, Wellingborough, Northants, 1987.

Markham, Ursula; *Discover Crystals*, Aquarian Press.

Mavor, James; *Voyage to Atlantis*, Putnam, New York, 1969.

Mitchell, John; *Secrets of the Stones*, Penguin, 1977.

Mitchell, John; *The View Over Atlantis*, Abacus, 1975.

Mitchell, John; *The New View Over Atlantis*, Harper & Row, 1983.

Mitchell-Hedges, F. A.; *Danger My Ally*, Pan Books, 1954.

Murray, M. (Dr); *The Splendour That Was Egypt*, Sidgwick and Jackson.

Neubert, Otto; *Tutankhamun*, Granada Publishing, New York, 1977.

Nielsen, Greg and Thoth; *Pyramid Power*, Warner Books, New York, USA, 1976.

Nielsen, Greg and Joseph Polansky; *Pendulum Power*, Aquarian Press, 1986.

Nyssa, Gregory; *The Life of Moses*, Paulist, New York, 1978.

Oldfield, Harry & Roger Coghill; *The Dark Side of the Brain*, Element Books, 1988.

Ozaniec, Naomi; *The Elements of The Chakras*, Element Books, 1990.

Palmer, Magda; *Healing Power of Crystals*, Arrow.

Randall-Stevens, H. C. (El Eros); *Atlantis to the Latter Days*, The Knights Templars of Aquarius, Jersey, 1981.

Raphael, Katrina; *Crystal Enlightenment*, Aurora Press, Santa Fe, New Mexico, USA, 1987.

Raphael, Katrina; *Crystalline Transmission*, Aurora Press, Santa Fe, New Mexico, USA, 1990.

Rea, John; *Healing & Quartz Crystals*, Two Trees Publishing, 1986.

Redford, Donald; *The Akhenaten Temple Project*, Aris & Phillip, 1976.

Redford, Donald; *Akhenaten: The Heretic King*, Princeton University Press, 1987.

Rolfe, Mona; *Initiation By The Nile*, C. W. Daniel, Saffron Walden, Essex, 1976.

Rolfe, Mona; *Radiation of the Light*, C. W. Daniel, Saffron Walden, Essex.

Rolfe, Mona; *The Sacred Vessel*, C. W. Daniel, Saffron Walden, Essex.

Rolfe, Mona; *The Spiral of Life*, C. W. Daniel, Saffron Walden, Essex.

Samson, Julia; *Amarna: City of Akhenaten and Nefertiti*, Aris and Phillip, 1978.

Saurat, D; *Atlantis and the Giants*, Faber and Faber.

Scott-Elliot, W; *Legends of Atlantis and Lost Lemuria*, Quest Books, 1990.

Scrutton, Robert; *The Message of the Masters*, Neville Spearman, 1982.

Sibley, Uma; *Complete Crystal Guide Book*, Bantam.

Simmons, Robert & Kathy Warner; *Moldavite, Starborn Stone of Transformation*, Heaven and Earth Books, 1988.

Smith, Michael; *Crystal Power*, Llewellyn Publications, St Paul, 1985.

Spence, Lewis; *Atlantis in America*, Ernest Benn Ltd, 1923.

Spence, Lewis; *The Problem of Atlantis*, William Rider, 1925.

Spence, Lewis; *Atlantis Discovered*, Causeway Books, 1974.

Spence, Lewis; *Myths and Legends of Ancient Egypt*, Farrar & Rinehart, New York, 1911.

Spence, Lewis; *Myths of Babylonia and Assyria*, George Garrap, 1916.

Spence, Lewis; *The History and Origins of Druidism*, Rider, 1942.

Spence, Lewis; *The Occult Sciences in Atlantis*, Rider, 1978.

Stearn, Jesse; *The Sleeping Prophet*, Frederick Muller, 1967.

Steiner, Rudolf; *Cosmic Memory: Atlantis and Lemuria*, Blouvelt, New York, 1959.

Szekely, Edmond Bordeaux; *The Gospel of the Essenes*, C. W. Daniel, Saffron Walden, Essex, 1978.

Szekely, Edmond Bordeaux; *The Teachings of the Essenes from Enoch to the Dead Sea Scrolls*, C. W. Daniel, Saffron Walden, Essex, 1978.

Tansley, David; *Chakras, Rays and Radionics*, C. W. Daniel, Saffron Walden, Essex, 1984.

Tansley, David; *Ray paths and Chakra Gateways*, C. W. Daniel, Saffron Walden, Essex, 1984.

Tansley, David; *Radionics and the Subtle Anatomy of Man*, C. W. Daniel, Saffron Walden, Essex.

Tomas, Andrew; *Atlantis: From Legend To Discovery*, Sphere Books, 1973.

Tompkins, Peter; *Secrets of the Great Pyramid*, Harper & Row, 1971.

Tompkins, Peter; *The Magic of the Obelisks*, Harper & Row, 1981.

Uriel & Antares; *Return To Atlantis*, Unarius Publications, 1992.

Uyldert, Mellie; *The Magic of Precious Stones*, Turnstone Press, Wellingborough, Northants, 1981.

Velikovsky, Immanuel; *Oedipus and Akhnaton*, Pocket Books, 1960.

Von Daniken, Erich; *Chariot Of The Gods*, Corgi Books.

Von Daniken, Erich; *Gold Of The Gods*, Corgi Books.

Von Daniken, Erich; *Return To The Stars*, Corgi Books.

Von Daniken, Erich; *In Search Of Ancient Gods*, Corgi Books.

Von Daniken, Erich; *Miracles Of The Gods*, Corgi Books.

Von Daniken, Erich; *Acccording To The Evidence*, Corgi Books.

Von Daniken, Erich; *The Stones of Kiribati*, Souvenir Press.

Von Daniken, Erich; *The Gods and their Grand Design*, Souvenir Press.

Walker, Barbara; *Book of Sacred Stones*, Harper Collins.

Walker, Dael; *The Crystal Book*, Sunol, California, USA, 1983.

Resource Directory

Colour Healing Therapists

Anson, Veronica, M.I.A.C.T., 'Lumiere', 7 Frankland Crescent, Poole, Dorset, BH14 9PX.

Bishop, Barbara, M.I.A.T.,M.Crys.H., 8 Woodcombe Cottages, Woodcombe, Minehead, Somerset, TA24 8SE.

Davidson, Jan, 67 Farm Crescent, Wexham Court, Slough, Berkshire, SL2 5TQ.

Fanthorpe, Kleo, Scarab, PO Box 77, West Kensington, London W14 0QQ.

Gimbel, Theo, Hygeia Studios, Avening, Tetbury, Gloucestershire.

Greenslade, Jean, 4 Sunningdale Close, Kirkham, Preston, Lancashire, PR4 2TG.

Greenslade, Tony, 4 Sunningdale Close, Kirkham, Preston, Lancashire, PR4 2TG.

Haigh, Joanne, M.I.A.C.T., 23 Brookfield Court, Burnage Avenue, Manchester, M19 2JB.

Hygeia Studios, Avening, Tetbury, Gloucestershire.

International Association for Colour Therapy, 73 Elm Bank
Gardens, Barnes, London, SW13 ONX.

Kemp, Veronica, Flat 2, 15 Malden Road, Watford, Herts,
WD1 3EN.

Lacey, Marie Louise, M.I.A.C.T., 3a Bath Road, Worthing,
Sussex, BN11 3NU.

Living Colour Association, 33 Lancaster Grove, London, NW3
4EX.

Maberley, Diana, M.I.A.C.T., Endellion, Money Row Green,
Holyport, Maidenhead, Berkshire, SL6 2NA.

Smith, Ruthie, 43b Mulkern Road, London, N19 3HQ.

Sun, Howard and Dorothy, 33 Lancaster Grove, London, NW3
4EX.

Universal Colour Healers Research Foundation, 67 Farm
Crescent, Wexham Court, Slough, Berkshire, SL2 5TQ.

Wills, Pauline, 9 Lyndale Avenue, Kingsbury, London, NW9.

All qualified colour healing therapists are entitled to become
members of the International Association for Colour Therapy.
The aims and objectives of the I.A.C.T. are:

1) To establish colour healing as a significant branch of
complementary therapy.
2) To determine professional standards of practice in the use of
colour.
3) To improve the understanding and use of colour in healing,
health, beauty, fashion, decor, industry and complementary
therapies.
4) To make it easier for people to find out more about colour
and how to avail themselves of colour therapy.

If you would like further information about Colour Therapy
please write to:

International Association for Colour Therapy
73 Elm Bank Gardens
Barnes
London SW13 ONX

The Living Colour Association

The living Colour Association is a non-profit making organisation established to promote health, healing and personal growth through colour.

The Aims of the L.C.A. are:

1) To promote colour awareness.
2) To establish the Living Colour approach as a valuable contribution to complementary medicine.
3) To provide a colour networking system for its members.
4) To study and research the use of colour and light.

Crystal Healing Therapists

United Kingdom

Abrahami, A. (Professor), Acu-Crystal Therapy Clinic, 35, Highview Avenue, Edgware, Middlesex, HA8 9TX.

Alexander, Mark, 2 Lilac Way, Quedgeley, Gloucester, GL2 6WH.

Askew, Marjorie, 26 Woodlands Drive, Hoole, Chester, CH2 3QH.

Ball, Chris, 30 Myddleton Lane, Winwick, Warrington, Cheshire, WA2 8NJ.

Barbasch, Audrey, D.O., 'Kerbar', 7 Rutland Road, Southport, Lancashire, PR8 6PB.

Bendon, Freddie, 10 Glen Crescent, Woodford Green, Essex, IG8 0AN.

Bowen, Michael, M.Crys.R., 105 Westfield Road, Edgbaston, Birmingham, West Midlands, B15 3JE.

Brydon, Christine, D.M.S. Astrol, C.Crys.T., 14 Southend Avenue, Darlington, Co. Durham, DL3 7HL.

Calligaro, Naomi, 'Rose Cottage', 6 High Street, Berkhamsted, Hertfordshire, HP4 2BS.

Carol, Lesley, 85a Lynton Road, Acton, London, W3 9BL.

Cawthorne, Constance, 53 Sicey Avenue, Sheffield,
Yorkshire, S5.

Clarke, Monica, 198 Middle Lane, London, N8 7LA.

Collins, Gillian, 5 Sunnymede Vale, Holcombe Brook, Bury,
Lancashire BL0 9RR.

Crowe, John, PO Box 1297, Halstead, Essex CO9 2LW.

Edmond, Catherine, 2 Margery Avenue, Scholars Green,
Stoke-on-Trent, Staffs, ST7.

Ellis, Margaret, M.R.T.A., 19 Fleming Way, Folkestone, Kent.

Fanthorpe, Kleo, Scarab, PO Box 77, West Kensington,
London, W14 0QQ.

Ford, Helen (Dr), The Hollies, 9 Redhill, Stourbridge,
West Midlands, DY3 1NA.

Forrester, David, 24 Myrtle Avenue, Eastcote, Ruislip,
Middlesex, HA4 8RZ.

Goodacre, Elizabeth, 11 Holdenby Road, Spratton, Northants
NN6 8JD.

'Great Life Crystal Healing Centre', 3/4 Moorview, Torpoint,
Cornwall PL11 2LH.

Gulliver, Peta, M.Crys.H., Lifeways, 2 Capondale Cottages,
New Lane, Holbrook, Suffolk, IP9 2RB.

Hampton, Pam, The Caring Clinic, 35 Barkers Road, Sheffield,
Yorkshire, S7 1SD.

Heaton, Irene, 83 Yew Tree Lane, West Derby, Liverpool,
Merseyside, L12 9HQ.

Henderson, Eric, North Star Crystals, 12 Cliff Boulevard,
Kimberley, Notts, NG16 2LB.

Hughes, Patricia, 128 Linton Rise, Cardale Estate,
Nottingham, NG3 7BZ.

Kermani, Kai (Dr), 10 Connaught Hill, Loughton, Essex,
IG10 4DU.

Kershaw, Wilf, C.Crys.T., Healing Hands, 204 Tinshill Lane,
Cookridge, Leeds, Yorkshire, LS16 7BL.

Keyte, Geoffrey, 37 Bromley Road, St Annes-on-Sea,
Lancashire, FY8 1PQ.
Khan, Jennifer, 9 Crebor Street, Dulwich, London, SE22 0HF.
Kingshott, Colin, 28 St. Marys Avenue, Barry Dock, Barry,
Glamorgan, Wales.
Lane, Annie, 5 Ernest Street, Cornholme, Todmorden,
Lancashire, OL14 8JS.
Light, Robert, 66 Tynewydd Road, Barry, South Glamorgan,
CF6 6BA.
Mathews, John, C.Crys.T., 2 Drewshead, Ilsington,
Newton Abbot, Devon, TQ13 9RG.
Mudge, June, 1 Terracina, Lower Erith Road, Torquay, Devon,
TQ1 2PX.
Mystical Crystal, 37 Bromley Road, St Annes-on-Sea,
Lancashire, FY8 1PQ.
Nalina, Constance, 12 Plover Close, Chatteris, Cambs,
PE16 6PP.
Pace, Pamela, Flight of the Phoenix, 3/4 Moor View, Torpoint,
Cornwall, PL11 2LH.
Powell, Maurice, 45 Old Church Lane, Stanmore, Middlesex,
HA7 2RG.
Scott-Cameron, John, 3a London Road, Crowborough,
East Sussex, TN6 2TT.
Simcock, Mary, 1 Percy Street, Amble, Morpeth,
Northumberland, NE65 0AG.
Skilton, Linda, 36 Haglane Copse, Pennington, Lymington,
Hants, SO41 8DR.
Squires, Premambika Sangita, Fishers Cottage, Sevenleaze
Lane, Edge, Gloucestershire.
Sugarman, John, 11 Golders Green Crescent, London,
NW11 8LA.
Trotta, Patrizia, 70 Allen Street, Maidstone, Kent, ME14 8AG.
Willcott, Corinne, 11 Albany Terrace, Leamington Spa,
Warwickshire, CV32 5ZP.

Wood, Valerie, 21 Streets Heath, West End, Woking, Surrey,
  GU24 9QY.
World Tree Mend Us, 17 Station Parade, Kew Gardens, Surrey.

Australia
Anderson, Philippa, 40 Couvreur Street, Garran, A.C.T.
  Australia 2065.

Canada
Andalaro, Ross, Natural Health Institute, 258 Dupont Street,
  Vancouver.
Brodie, Renee, 548 English Bluff Road, Delta, B.C.
  V4M 2N3, Canada.
Grey, Lahane, Suite 109, 2045 Barclay Street, Vancouver,
  Canada, V6R 2J3.
Loh, Joseph Wiona, 1255 Bidwell Street, Apt 2309, Vancouver,
  Canada, V6G 2K8.

France
Baudry, Frederic, Institut de Critallo Therapie, La Marie Fee,
  Chemin de la Galante, 83340 Le Cannet des Maures, France.
Singleton, Maggie, Les Amourenes, 83690 Salemes, Var
  France.

Hawaii
Chu, Cynthia, 1521 Punahou Ste 1301, Honolulu, Hawaii
  96822.

Netherlands
Brandt, A. C. (Mrs), Nettelaorsterweg 6, 7241 Pk Lochem,
  The Netherlands.
Jansen, Fred, De Oorsprang, Verkuyl Quakkelaastraat 105,
  4381, TL Vlissingen, The Netherlands.

Northern Ireland
Burgess, Jacquie, Slaney House, Barrack Street, Tullow,
County Carlow, Northern Ireland.

Singapore
Loh, Meeling, 24 Poh Huat Road, Singapore 1954.
Sim, Andy (Dr), 24 Poh Huat Road, Singapore 1954.

Sri Lanka
Perera, Roy, 'Birdlyn', 167 Kotugoda Road, Seeduwa,
Sri Lanka.

USA
Bazinet, Rozanne (Dr), PO Box 662005, Sacramento,
CA 95866, USA.
Boddie, Caroline, 65 Brighton Street, Rochester, NY 14607,
USA.
Bonito, Salvatore, 333 West 5th Street, New York, NY 10019,
USA.
Crystal Palace, 14201 Bodega Hwy, Bodega, California 94922,
USA.
Fern, Shyla, 16022 Moor Park, Encino, CA 91436, USA.
Gosse, Jean, 2407 Camino Capitan, Sante Fe, NM 87505, USA.
Hanham, Connie, PO Box 467, Woodstock, NY 12498, USA.
Keyte, Geoffrey, The Mystical Crystal, 217 Park Avenue,
Box 332, Worcester, MA 01609-2243, USA.
Nocerino, F. R. 'Nick', PO Box 302, Pinole, California 94564,
USA.
Ojela, Frank, 8 Windmill Lane, New York, NY 10956, USA.
Pyradyne Inc, 1278 Glenneyre #255, Laguna Beach, VA 92651,
USA.
Quintaria, Cherokee, PO Box 5874, Santa Fe, New Mexico
87502, USA.

Robinson, Lindsay, 2532 Camino Estribo, Santa Fe, New
Mexico 87505, USA.
Sleby, Peter, 426 W. Cleveland, Bozeman, Montana 59715,
USA.
Society of Crystal Skulls, PO Box 302, Pinole, California 94564,
USA.
Tragg, Jeff, 22 N E 11th Street, Gainesville, Florida 32601, USA.
Welsh, Samuel, 9714 Brent Street, Manassas, VA 22110, USA.

Crystal Shops/Stores

United Kingdom
Arcturus Books & Crystals, 47 Fore Street, Totnes, Devon,
TQ9 5NJ.
Aristia, Royal Albert Walk, Albert Road, Southsea, Hants,
PO4 0JT.
Artisan, 3 King Street, Delph, Nr. Oldham, Lancashire,
OL3 5DL.
Crystal Dawn, 19a Quennevais Parade, St Brelade, Jersey,
Channel Islands, JE3 8FX.
Earthlore, 14 Fore Street, Hexham, Northumberland,
NE46 1ND.
Enchanted, 22 Harris Arcade, Reading, Berkshire, RG11.
Enigma, 100 Old Christchurch Road, Bournemouth, Dorset,
BH1 1LR.
Fossils, 35 Park Hill, Shirehampton, Bristol, Avon, BS11 0UH.
Gemini Gems, 53 High Street, Chobham, Woking, Surrey,
GU24 8AF.
Health Matters, 39 Cotham Hill, Cotham, Bristol, Avon,
BS6 6JY.
Human Nature, 12 South Street, Dorking, Surrey, RH4 2HQ.
Kernow Fossils and Minerals, An-Velyn Seaureaugh,
St. Stythyans, near Truro, Kernow, Cornwall.

North Star (Mail Order only), 12 Cliff Boulevard, Kimberley,
   Notts, NG16 2LB.
Rock Warehouse, PO Box 602, Ilford, Essex, IG3 8EP.
   (Wholesale only)
Stellar Gateway, 21 Carlton Place, Southampton, Hants
   SO15 2DY.
Tideswell Dale Rock Shop, Commercial Road, Tideswell,
   Derbyshire, SK17 8NU.
Winfalcon Healing Centre, 28/29 Ship Street, Brighton,
   Sussex, BN1 1AD.
Wood Matters, 12a Brecknock Road, London, N7 0DD.
World Tree, 17k Station Parade, Kew Gardens, Surrey, TW9 3PS.

Australia

Adyar Bookshop, 16 Anderson Street, Sydney Chatswood 2067,
   Australia.
Aquarian Books and Crystals, 127 York Street, Sydney,
   Australia.
Fascinating Facets, 69 Main Street, Atherton, QLD 4883,
   Australia.
Gemcraft, 14 Duffy Street, Burwood, Victoria 3125, Australia.

Canada

Avenue Lapidary Supplies, 873 Portage Avenue, Winnipeg,
   MB, Canada, R3G 0N8.
Canadian Natural Crystal Company, 6120-2nd St. S.E.,
   Suite A-23, Calgary AB, Canada.
Crystal Import International, Box 461, 810 W. Broadway,
   Vancouver, B.C. V5Z 4C9, Canada.
Crystal Works, PO Box 35231, Station 'E', Vancouver, B.C.
   V6M 4G4, Canada.
Green's Rock & Lapidary Ltd, 1603 Centre Street North,
   Calgary, Alberta, T2E 2S2, Canada.

Rainbow Minerals, 5470 Canotek Road, Unit 26, Gloucester,
Ontario, Canada, K1J 9A9.
Rock Cut Gems Inc., 147a Main Street, Unionville, Ontario,
Canada, L3R 2G8.

Denmark
Hedegaard, Storgade 71-M, DK-8882, Faarvang, Denmark.

Holland
Gemstone Remedies, Zandkamp, 313 NL-3828, GV Hoogland,
The Netherlands.
Mesoliet Groothandel in Halfedelstene, Hooftstraat 327c,
Alphen A/D RIJN, The Netherlands.

India
Fair Gem India, 12 Tulip, 3rd Pasta Lane, Colaba, Bombay
400 005, India.
Zeolites India, D-311 Manju Mahal, 35 Nargis Dutt Road,
Bandra, W. Bombay 400 050, India.

Sri Lanka
Astor Jewellery Ltd, 728 Galle Road, Colombo 3, Sri Lanka.
Gem Ray Ltd, Shop No. 4, Hotel Lanka Oberoi, Colombo 3,
Sri Lanka.
Premadass & Co (Jewellers) Ltd, Commercial House,
30 Duke Street, Colombo 1, Sri Lanka.
State Gem Corporation, 25 Galle Face Terrace, Colombo 3,
Sri Lanka.

USA
Academy of Living Light, 374 Woodfield Road, W. Hempstead,
New York 11552.
Allen's Rocks, 26513 Center Ridge Road, Cleveland, OH
44145.

Arizona Gems & Minerals, 6370 E. Highway 69, Prescott Valley,
AZ 86314.
Ark, 133 Romero Street, Santa Fe, NM 87501.
Asthetic Lapidary & Gift House, 32 State Street, Bangor,
ME 04401.
Aum Kara Bookstore, 1314 Union Avenue, N.E., Renton,
WA 98056.
Aurora Mineral Corporation, 16 Niagara Avenue, Freeport,
NY 11520.
B & J Rock Shop, 620 Claymont Estates Dr, Ballwin, MO 63001.
Barbera Company, 1038 Regent Street, Alameda, CA 94501.
Blue Ridge Rock Shop, Rt. 1, Box 811, Spruce Pine, NC 28777.
Bruce's Rock Shop, PO Box 237, Hwy. 90W, Hondo, TX 78861.
Carousel Gems, 1202 Perion Dr, Belen, NM 87002.
Cheshire Moon, Westmeadow Plaza, 164 Milk Street,
Westboro, MA 01581.
China West Gems, 803 Main Street, Lake Geneva, WI 53147.
Colorado Gem & Mineral Co, PO Box 424, Tempe, AZ 85281.
Columbine Mineral Shop, 633 Main Street, Ouray, CO 81427.
Crystal Cluster, 510 Kelly Avenue, Half Moon Bay, CA 94019.
Crystal Deva Designs, PO Box 1445, Santa Fe, N.M.
87504-1445.
Crystal Essence, 40 Railroad Street, Great Barrington,
MA 01230.
Crystal Fountain, PO Box 169, Royal Arkansas 71968.
Crystal Import International, Box 3439, Blaine, Washington,
98230.
Crystal Moon, PO Box 580, Belmont, CA 94002.
Crystal Oracle, 51 Morton Street, New York, NY 10014.
Crystal Store, 7320 Ashcroft, Suite 303, Houston, TX 77081.
Crystal Voyage, 315 Gregory Street, Rochester, NY 14620.
Cureton Mineral Co, PO Box 5761, Tucson, AZ 85703.
David Shannon Minerals, 1727 W. Drake Circle, Mesa,
AZ 85202.

Dick's Rock Shop, 7310 South Hwy, 85-87 Fountain, CO 80817.
Dyck's Minerals, 1559N. 18th St, Laramie, WY 82070.
Earth Magic, Inc, 205 East Fourth, Olympia, WA 98501.
Frances' Stones, 13101 Spring Run Road, Midlothian,
    VA 23113.
Gemini Minerals, PO Box 52, Tipp City, OH 45371.
Heaven & Earth, PO Box 224, Marshfield, VT 05658.
Horizon Mineral Company, 13765 Sablecrest, Houston,
    TX 77014.
Hutsell's Rock Shop, 606 South 16th, Blue Springs, MO 64015.
Jayhawk Rock Shop, 116 W. Main Street, Box 296, Hill City,
    KS 67642.
Jewel Tunnel Imports, PO Box 267, Arcadia, CA 91006-0267.
Kal Rock & Minerals, PO Box 1914, Rock Springs,
    WY 82902.
Karma Crystal, 662 East Kossuth Street, Columbus, Ohio
    43206.
Krystal Haven, PO Box 331389, Fort Worth, TX 76163.
Lucky Strike Rock Shop, 283 N. Washington Street, Plainville,
    CT 06062.
Magical Rocks, 19 Monmouth Street, Red Bank, NJ 07701.
Michigan Lapidary Supply Co, 29845 Beck Road, Wixem,
    MI 48096.
Miracles Unlimited, 81 Central Avenue, Wailuku, Maui, Hawaii
    96793.
Muston Rock Shop, 300 N. Bickford, El Reno, OK 73036.
Mystical Crystal, 217 Park Avenue, Box 332, Worcester,
    MA 01609-2243.
New Age Concepts, PO Box 12, 8972 East Hampden Avenue,
    Denver, CO 80231.
New Age Vibrations, 1840 So. Gaffey Street, San Pedro,
    CA 90731.
Packard's Rock Shop, 13131 Midlothian Turnpike, PO Box 10,
    Midlothian, VA.

Red & Green Minerals, 7595 W. Florida Ave, Lakewood,
CO 80226.

Rockbottom Minerals, Box 291, Madison, IN 47250.

Sevier Rock Shop, Rt 9, Barnett Circle Road, Knoxville,
TN 37920.

Sierra Contact Minerals, 1002 S. Wells Avenue, Reno,
NV 89502.

Sierra Vista Minerals, 2375 E. Tropicana, Las Vegas, NV 89119.

Skyline Rock Shop, 3939 Skyline Drive, Rapid City, SD 57702.

Spencer Gem & Lapidary Shop, 1624 Potomac Avenue,
Lafayette, IN 47905.

Talisman Trading Company, PO Box 1895, La Mesa, CA 92041.

Thunderbird Rocks, 3510 Schofield Ave, Schofield, WI 54476.

Topaz Gem & Mineral Shop, 942 Pearl Street, Boulder,
CO 80302

Touch of Magic, PO Box 46, Fairfax, CA 94930.

V Rock Shop, 4760 Portaga St. NW, North Canton,
OH 44720.

Volcano Rock Shop, 1600 Dunlap, Mission, TX 78572.

West Germany
Kristalldruse, Oberanger 6, D-8000, Munich 2, West Germany.

Sound Therapists

United Kingdom
Alexander, Mark, 2 Lilac Way, Quedgeley, Gloucester,
GL2 6VM.

Allen, W. (Dr), 3 Hocroft Road, West Hampstead, London.

Barber, Valerie, 15 Redcroft Drive, Erdington, Birmingham,
West Midlands.

Bell, Douglas, 2 Wheatfield Road, Ayr, Scotland, KA7 2XR.

Chilkes, Jayne, 12a Vista Drive, Redbridge, Essex, IG4 8JE.

Clarke, Monica, 198 Middle Lane, London, N8 7LA.

Collins, Brian, 63 Garret Street, Attleborough, Nuneaton, Warwickshire.

Crowe, John, PO Box 1297, Halstead, Essex, CO9 2LW.

Edmond, Catherine, 2 Margery Avenue, Scholar Green, Stoke-on-Trent, Staffs, ST7

Ford, H., 18 Marlborough Place, Wimbourne, Dorset.

Fraser, Judy, 2 Oakhurst, Balcombe Road, Haywards Heath, Sussex, RH16 1PD.

George (Mrs), 123 Pershore Road, Edgbaston, Birmingham, West Midlands.

Gooding, Nigel (Dr), 21 Alma Road, Reigate, Surrey.

Harrison (Mrs), 114 Windermere Road, Kendal, Cumbria, LA9 1VZ.

Holmes, D. (Mrs), 6 Mill Avenue, Broadway, Worcestershire.

Jackson, H. (Dr), 26 Redlands Road, Reading, Berkshire, RG11 5EX.

Johnstone, M. (Mrs), 7 Cakebridge Road, Cheltenham, Glos.

Kershaw, Wilf, Healing Hands, 204 Tinshill Lane, Cookridge, Leeds, Yorkshire LS16.

Lane, Annie, 5 Ernest Street, Cornholme, Todmorden, Lancashire, OL14 8JS.

Lings, Georgie, 37 King Edward Street, Scunthorpe, South Humberside, DN16.

Manners, Peter Guy, M.D., D.O., Bretforton Hall, Bretforton, Evesham, Worcestershire, WR11 5JH.

Matushita, Y., 55 Hampden Road, Harrow Weald, Middlesex HA3 8PS.

Melrose, C. J. (Mr/Mrs), Sayes Court Lodge, Liberty Lane, Addlestone, Surrey.

Miller, Ian, 12 Kingswood Close, Merrow, Guildford, Surrey, GU1 2SD.

Pace, Pamela, Flight of the Phoenix, 3/4 Moor View, Torpoint, Cornwall, PL11 2LH.

Paige, Rita, 20a Kenmere Gardens, Wembley, Middlesex,
  HA0 1TE.
Parker, Rosamund, 4 Royal Road, Ramsgate, Kent,
  CT11 9LE.
Poole, Pauline, 3 Temple Close, Hadleigh, Essex.
Reick, R. (Dr), 4 Craigpark, Dennistoun, Glasgow, Scotland,
  G31 2NA.
Rudd, Philip, 10 Gissing Road, Burston, Diss, Norfolk,
  IP22 3UD.
Salt, P. (Mrs), 50 Lynch Road, Farnham, Surrey.
Sansbury, Vera, 26 Ashleigh Road, Solihull, West Midlands,
  B91 1AF.
Shepard, David, 150 High Street, Burford, Oxfordshire.
Taylor, Jean, 18 Long Reach Road, Chesterton, Cambridge
  CB4 1UH.
Terry, Peter, Tickenhill Manor, Park Lane, Bewdley,
  Worcestershire, DY12 2ER.
Vick, Paul, 90 Dumbarton Road, London, SW2.
Wade, P. (Mrs), Willow Cottage, Stockland Green Road,
  Tunbridge Wells, Kent, TN3 0TL.
Williams (Mrs), 5 Bourne Road, Kingskerswell, Newton Abbot,
  Devon.
Wright, A (Mrs), West Balscalloch, Kirkcolm Stranraer,
  Wigtownshire.

Ireland
McManus, Margaret, 81 Bayside Boulevard North, Sutton,
  Dublin 13, Ireland.

USA
Centrepoint Research Institute, 4470, Southwest Hall Blvd,
  Suite 173, Beaverton, OR 97005, USA.
Halpem, Steven, Sound RX, PO Box 2644, San Anselmo,
  CA 94979, USA.

New Age Products Co, PO Box 7771, Milwaukee, WI 53207, USA.

Shulman, Richard, PO Box 467, Woodstock, NY 12498, USA.

Gem Elixirs

The Dr Reckeweg Electroacupuncture Apparatus referred to in Chapter 14 is available from Frank Eastwood, 39 Browns Lane, Coventry, West Midlands, CV5 9DT.

A comprehensive range of flower essences are also available.

Further information on the subject of gem elixirs will be included in Frank Eastwood's forthcoming book entitled Gem Elixirs and Bioenergetic medicine.

For details and syllabuses of courses arranged by Frank Eastwood and those he is running in conjunction with Crystal 2000, please write to him at the address above.

Index